LET'S SKIP TO THE GOOD BITS!

A shocking account of a brutal knife attack and the courageous 20-year battle to getting one man's life back.

Darren Barden

Orders: Please contact - www.darrenbarden.com

You can also order via the e mail address –
dbauthor67@gmail.com

ISBN: 978-1-5272-2162-8

First published 2018

Copyright © 2018 Darren Barden. All rights reserved.

CONTENTS

"21 years on from the biggest event in my life, I have finally got myself to a place where I can write intimately about what life has been like for me and my family, since it happened. I am no different from anybody else who has suffered a life changing trauma, but I want to share with you the impact that trauma can have, and the way it can change so many things and so many people, both directly and indirectly."

Dedicated to

This book is dedicated to my wife Wendy. Without your love and support, I simply would not be here today.

ACKNOWLEDGEMENTS

I would like to take this opportunity to thank everyone involved in the writing of this book and in the publication. I was lucky enough to have an email sent to my wife Wendy by mistake, where I was invited to join a FREE – yes FREE – book writing seminar, where a guy called Richard McMunn was going to tell us all how to write and self-publish a book. Attending this seminar was one of the most important decisions I have ever made. It sent me on the path to having this book completed, so thank you Richard McMunn.

I would also like to thank everyone who has contributed with their thoughts. Although my own thoughts, feelings and experiences form the bulk of this book, it's always great to gain some outside perspective on what happened. Trauma doesn't just impact you, but everyone around you too. There are too many individuals for me to thank, so I will keep it to a very few, who have not only been there for me in the past, but are still here for me now:

My mum and dad (Pete & Sue) who for many years have supported me and my family in ways that only parents could do. I hope that when they read this book they can sit back and say they helped, and see that I have really moved on and "skipped to the good bits".

My 2 wonderful children, George and Shannon. They understand me, and support me, despite all of the things they have witnessed and lived through. Shannon has taken on the role of helping me promote my book and all the other activities I am getting involved in, as a consequence of writing the book. Shannon has also built my website, which I am very happy with.

Each and every single member of my family, who have listened to me going on about everything, and nodded politely and smiled where needed. Teresa, Janet, Kath, and my late Grandad – who gave us all the moral guidance to be good, honest, family people.

My friends, who have supported me through good and bad times, and kept a smile on my face when times were hard. Thank you to Stuart and Rachel, Deb McGhee and Rob Hurst, plus Pete and Jo who were also there in the early stages of my financial fallout.

There has also been a guy in my life for many years now, and without him I may not have had the strength to get through various jobs in the past. Clive Jones was and still is an inspirational bloke to me and possibly others as well. Over the past 5 years Clive has undergone his own battles in life following a brain tumour, but I would like to take this opportunity to say thank you, Clive. Thank you for always being there when there were very few people who understood what I was going through.

I would also like to thank my current employer Hilti GB and my work colleagues, because without me joining Hilti I would never have reached a position of contentment in my work, and so may never have written this book.

Thank you to my Auntie Kath who has taken the time to write the forward for me, which I can imagine was not an easy task. Kath has been a source of support to me and my family over the years, whilst building a very successful career in nursing. This was finally recognised when Kath won Clinical Nurse of 2017, after years of dedication to her industry.

Just after the event I was helped by Victim Support, and in particular a lady called Ronnie Ayers. She felt that 12 months after the attack I should write a book about my experience. Well, 21 years later I have done it. Thank you, Ronnie.

I have been fortunate enough to meet new people whilst writing this book and Steph Shilton is one of those people. I would like to say a big thank you to Steph for taking the time to contribute by writing about the charity MIND and her work with them.

Finally, to my wife Wendy – thank you. You have saved my life. I know you can't see it, but just putting this down in words makes me cry tears of both joy and happiness. You are the most important person in my world.

FOREWORD BY KATHY WADHAMS

This book is about my nephew, the struggles he has faced and the challenges this has brought for an ordinary man, who has now become an extraordinary man. It explains the problems he has faced, and how he has overcome a lot of fears with humour.

I remember the night this attack happened, it changed my nephew at the time and had a terrible impact on our family. The details were too horrific to take in at first, but as it slowly unravelled it sickened me. The way someone can knock on the door of a stranger, without knowing their identity, and attack them in such a depraved way while a wife and small baby lay upstairs, is beyond comprehension.

There was never any justice, and nobody was caught. This has added to the long-term effects brought upon this family, which were for many years a burden. I believe that this makes Darren's story even more admirable.

He eventually lost his house, his job and without his ever-supportive wife Wendy and Victim Support he would have lost his mental health forever. Victim Support are an independent charity, who have been running for 40 years and partly rely on donations. They were a resource that Darren continually pulled on in his hour of need.

The justice system gets less than 5% of government spending, and less than 1p from every £1 of the Ministry of Justice budget is spent on victims and witnesses directly. This low level of funding does not reflect a low level of need: more than one in five victims wants some form of support, but at least three in ten do not get the support they need.

It is thought that those who have had contact with Victim Support have more confidence in the Criminal Justice System, are more likely to think that the police do an excellent job, have a greater satisfaction with the police's handling of their case, and greater trust in the fairness of the Criminal Justice System.

(www.victimsupport.org.uk)

Despite dealing with his own problems, Darren has helped others with their own struggles. He has attended help groups, presenting and discussing his experiences. For a while he even worked as a volunteer for Victim Support, and organised fundraising events for them as well. He also appeared on a talk show *Kilroy* many years ago, in which he discussed his experience, all with the aim of overcoming his own anxiety and helping others.

My nephew has written this book to help other ordinary people who have endured something horrific in their lives, so that they may gain something back from reading about Darren's experience. This could have happened to any of us...but it happened to him, my nephew. He is a great man, caring, courageous and funny, and I consider myself lucky to have him in my life. Even though over the years he has faced a lot of demons, he is always there helping others, with a sense of humour.

Over the course of 21 years, Darren's physical scars have healed, but the mental scars will never fully disappear. This book is a frank account of someone's actual struggle to recover from a savage attack, and how humour can lift even the lowest of spirits.

My nephew is an inspiration to me, and I truly hope that his words and wisdom can help you too.

Kathleen Wadhams – DIP HE , RGN, Clinical Nurse award 2017

PREFACE

My wish is that anyone who reads this book can find something they relate to, either emotionally or compassionately. I would like people to understand that whatever the cause of trauma in your life, you can get through it. This is not a self-help book, and I am no doctor. I am just a normal fella, who wants to share his story, in the hope that you or someone you know can take inspiration from me, and change the future.

We would all like a nice simple life, full of happiness and fun, but most of the time it doesn't quite turn out that way. During our journey there are some huge obstacles which can knock you off course, and make happiness seem abstract and out of reach. I hope that my story will encourage you to keep going, and realise that happiness can come in many forms and levels. We can all have happiness – so please let me help you to find yours.

During the writing of this book, I have learnt many things about a lot of people, and some of those things really took me by surprise. I have learnt about how one terrifying night for myself has haunted those closest to me. I have learnt about how people did not know how to deal with the situation, and the subsequent fallout from that night.

I have learnt that there are more people out there suffering from a mental illness, because of things that may or may not have been under their control. But most of all, I have learnt that I really have come out of the other end – intact, surviving, and am now enjoying every day of my life, just because I can.

CHAPTER 1

My Normal World

I am pleased to say that my childhood was one of fond memories, and I can only remember fun and happiness. As a family, we were no different to most in our area. We had very little money, but somehow my mum and dad managed to always put food on the table and clothes on our backs. Even if it meant sleeping in the back of one of my dad's work vans, we always had a holiday. My dad was a lorry driver, and my mum was a school dinner lady, before eventually becoming a cook at Westminster Abbey School in London.

I started my school life at Little Parndon Primary School, which according to my mum I hated. Every day on the way to school I would scream my head off, coming up with all sorts of plans as to why I should not go. Once my parents were offered a council house in a new housing estate on the other side of town, things improved for me. This is where most of my childhood memories begin. I started at Milwards Primary and Junior School, and then progressed on to Stewards Senior School in Staple Tye. Despite my habit of bunking off and messing about, I generally enjoyed my time there, and to this day remain in touch with some of my friends from that school. Unfortunately, I left school with very little to my name, and a set of words ringing in my ears:

"You will amount to nothing, Mr. Barden, if you do not change."

Back then, I had dreams of becoming a graphic designer. Through sheer hard work and determination, and over 200 hundred letters to many companies and organisations, I managed to land myself an apprenticeship – via what was called the YTS (Youth Training Scheme) as a sign writer.

I started work on the YTS in 1984, working for a company called Stone Signs. I worked there for 8 years, and enjoyed some fantastic relationships. It was during this time, in my opinion, that I grew into a man. The owners of the business were great, and if they were all still here then I would thank them for taking me into their family. I can only hope that someone may read this and pass my thoughts on to them or their families. So, to Terry Bird, Tony and Lesley McCabe, thank you. Likewise, thank you to Bob Williams, Kevin Hickman and Ginger (Ken) Dixon – who was one of the most talented sign writers I have ever met.

It was during this period that I met my wife of 27 years (at the time of writing), Wendy. I used to drink in my local pub, The Herald, most days of the week – doing all the things that young men did at that time. Wendy's parents, Babs and Herby, ran the pub, and it just so happened that one day Wendy was there, cleaning glasses. It was a window of opportunity I could not miss. They only ran the pub for around 6 months, so I was extremely lucky.

I had overheard Wendy having a conversation with her mum about a family party they were going to that weekend. Being a keen party goer, I decided to try and get in on the act. After hours of relentless questioning, I eventually conceded defeat and had to wait for another day. This was not to be too far away. I managed to convince Wendy to go out on a date with me to another local pub, where a band I knew were playing. The pub was called The Three Horseshoes and if I remember correctly the guy singing in the band was called Eddie Vincent. This was to be our first proper date! We spent the whole evening looking across the table at each other in silence, as the music was so bloody loud we couldn't have a conversation.

Several of the previous landlords from The Herald had barred me for childish pranks, like stacking pint glasses on the table many levels high and trying to remove one from the bottom of the pile, but Herby was having none of my antics, and quickly brought me in line.

After 2 years of going out with each other, I decided to ask Wendy to get engaged. I wanted to do this in the proper fashion, so I asked if she could arrange for me to meet her dad and ask for his daughter's hand in marriage. Wendy was so excited she promptly went home and told her dad we were getting engaged. BIG mistake! Herby responded with, "I don't think so" and to be fair he was right. His opinion was that, since we were going away to Tenerife for 2 weeks soon, we should see if we could spend those weeks together in a small room. If we came back and still felt the same then we would have his blessing. Two weeks' later, we returned from holiday, still very much in love. To my relief, Herby relented, and we were officially engaged.

In typical Darren fashion, I wanted a big party to tell the world that we were getting engaged, so that is what we did. By this time Babs and Herby had taken over the Conservative Club in Hoddesdon, Hertfordshire, which had a marvellous hall and facilities that we made good use of.

2 years after our engagement, we got married. The day of the wedding was exactly 4 years on from our very first date, July 14th 1990. It was a great traditional family event. The ceremony took place at St Mary Magdalene Church, and we had the reception at the Harlow Rugby Club. When I look back on that day it always fills me with happiness, and it remains one of the greatest days of my life.

Through a sheer stroke of luck, we were then given the opportunity to move to New Zealand. The invite came from Chris Porter, son of Geoff and Liz, who were my mum and dad's friends from yesteryear. We made all the plans, got ourselves ready… and I promptly ruined it by breaking my leg playing football on a Sunday.

Still, not one for being put off, we rearranged the dates and eventually arrived in Auckland in March of 1992. What a great trip that was. We met some fantastic people, who are still very good friends of ours. Simon Porter was one such friend, he took us into his world and introduced us to some brilliant people, including Dean and Fiona Jackson – two of the finest individuals you could ever wish to meet. Tragically, Simon lost his life at the age of 31, and to this day he is sorely missed by everyone who was lucky enough to know him.

On 30th August 1992 we moved to Australia, to live with my Uncle Eddie. To say that this was an experience would be an understatement. Australia was full of activities that were alien to me and Wendy, but once again gave us the opportunity to meet some incredible characters. This included Wayne (The Shark Bite) and Del (The Honey Monster). We also met one of the most generous people I have ever known: Mad Mal from Muswell Hill. What a guy! Malcolm was mad and as it happens originally from Muswell Hill in London. He would have us laughing for hours and hours with his anecdotes and jokes. I would love to tell you about all of our adventures in Australia, but I might have to save that for another book.

To earn my way in Australia I had a spell delivering antiques with my

2 uncles for the Australian Antiques Roadshow, and then moving people's homes around Sydney. I also took part in some debt-collecting for various agencies out there, but eventually it was time to come home. We arrived back in England in December 1992. Wendy's mum and dad picked us up from the airport and drove us back to my parents' house in Potter Street, Harlow. It was at this point that our lives really began, from a normal point of view. I went back to driving a van, Wendy got a job with General Portfolio as an Insurance Administrator, and on we went.

On September 13th 1995, our son George was born. By the age of 3 months he had developed an illness which affected his immune system, and over the course of 2 years we nearly lost him about 4 times. There was a particular part of his immune system that was weak. Most people would have been measured at about 12 to 14 out of 19, but George had a reading of 3. This meant that every time George would get a cold it would very rapidly turn to Bronchial Pneumonia, and thus end up with George in a hospital bed, with ventilators and pipes coming out of his little baby body. Together, we came through this, although it was mostly down to the strength of Wendy that we did so. George has since made a full recovery, and has been perfectly fit and healthy since he was 4 years old.

As I said earlier, I really was no different to most people when growing up and starting out my adult life. However, this was all set to change...

The House, 101 Brockles Mead

Through a longstanding friend of mine, an opportunity came up to buy a house that he had previously rented out. Harvey was a hard-working businessman, who was pretty much a self-made millionaire. Harvey's parents had been friends with my parents even before we were born, so we knew each other well. Harvey had been having some trouble in this house with drug dealers and takers, and was struggling to get rent from the tenants.

Harvey relied on his close friend Dan to collect any outstanding rents. Trust me, when Dan darkened your door there was always a solution, so Harvey got his money. After regular complaints from the neighbours about the tenants in this house, and almost daily police or Dan visits, Harvey decided to empty the address of all residents. One in particular ended up being arrested and sentenced to several years in prison, so that tells you about the kind of character who had been renting this house!

101 Brockles Mead had been empty for about 18 months when Wendy and I decided to buy it for £36,900. Harvey used his solicitors, and handled everything for us, which I think suited Harvey for the movement of money. In the 18 months since Harvey kicked out the previous tenants, the house had been damaged by burglars, who kept breaking in hoping to find something worth stealing – bad luck there. So, naturally, it was a mess from the ground up. We spent the first couple of months not living there, but just cleaning away the mess, which included needles and human waste. We replaced everything, the floors, ceilings, toilets, windows. This was hindered by several attempts to put a stop to our hard work, through vandalism and more attempts to break in.

One unfortunate young lad decided to scribe his initials into the walls, and on the external drain pipes. After asking around, I discovered who "NS" was, and went to knock on their door. As you can imagine, the parents of "NS" were in denial at first. However, after encouraging the parents to come over and see for themselves, they promptly went away to deal with the boy. We later had the boy knock on our door, apologise, and offer to help with any clearing up. It's a shame that this is no longer an option in current British society.

I always felt as if there was something dodgy going on at 101 Brockles Mead. My post box was full of brown envelopes (not belonging to me), which contained DSS cheques to various people. So, twice a week I would call Harvey, and Dan would turn up in his black leather jacket to collect the envelopes. Dan is sadly no longer with us, but he was a really nice guy, just as long as you were paying what you owed or in my case adding to the ever-growing empire of Harvey. Back in the mid-90s, a thousand pounds was an awful lot of money. I would estimate that on a regular basis there was well over a grand being collected some weeks.

At the point of buying 101, Wendy and I had planned to spend the next 2 years re-developing the property into a family home. Almost immediately after signing for 101, Wendy fell pregnant, so our 2-year plan was rapidly accelerated. We moved walls, replaced ceilings, and fairly quickly this derelict property became a very tidy 4-bedroom family home – just in time for Wendy to arrive back from hospital with George.

Like most people in our world, we were struggling to make ends meet. To keep up our new investment, I would work Monday to Friday daytime, and to earn extra money I would work nights delivering newspapers to the shops before they opened.

What a job that was. Everyone there was only doing it because they were skint, so the atmosphere was a little bit fiery to say the least. People were tired, pissed off and poor, and sparks would fly as well as fists. Almost every day there was a punch-up caused by people stacking papers in someone else's spot, or parking where they knew it would piss someone off.

There was one particular night, where myself and a man named Eric Golding were helping each other pack up our papers for our rounds, when a huge row started about 30 feet away from where we were working. It was incredible! Blokes from all across the factory rushed over, took sides and joined in, but Eric and I just looked at each other, used this as an opportunity to jump the now missing queue, and get out of there. The language was less than friendly, and these guys were throwing punches and bundles of newspapers at each other, but Eric and I just jumped in our vans and left them to it.

The funny part is that everyone would turn up for their next shift and the previous night's events would never get mentioned. I just got my head down every night, and in the main avoided any fracases. By this point in my life, I think it's fair to say that I was beginning to mature. Old me would have jumped straight into the aforementioned fracas, but now I was wise enough not to make decisions that would risk my livelihood.

Also working the newspaper round was a guy called Vic – an old-fashioned ducker and diver. Vic will appear later in this book, as he was to play a small part in my story.

Because of this job, I was generally in bed before 8pm every night. The shifts used to start at 2am, Sunday to Thursday and midnight Friday and Saturday. In a strange way though, I enjoyed that job. There was a real benefit to doing it, even with the anti-social hours and the fights, and the poor pay – just £150 a week. At the end of the day, it gave my son a good start to life, and for that reason I will always be grateful for it.

CHAPTER 2

A Knock on the Door

The 7th October 1996 was a Monday. It was a slightly different Monday, as it was the very last day of my job as a multidrop van driver with one company. I was due to start a new same-day delivery job, with Shepherds Transport, on Tuesday.

At some point that day, I found myself in the middle of a situation. I was at the junction of the A12 and the A406 Redbridge in London. A Volkswagen Beetle suddenly stopped at the roundabout when it was clear to go, and a Peugeot behind it banged into the back of the Beetle. I in turn banged into the back of the Peugeot. For some reason, the Beetle just drove off, leaving me and a very nervous Indian guy sorting out the prang. The Indian man's boot was unable to close, but he was adamant that it wasn't a problem. He said that it was his brother's car, so wanted no fuss, and was happy to drive off without giving over any details. As you know, the vehicle that goes into the back is normally the one to take the blame, but with no damage to my van I was happy to complete my last day.

Early that evening I drove over to Bishops Stortford, to collect my new van in preparation for my new start. I parked the van outside my house. As always, I was in bed before 8pm, as I was still delivering papers to shops for the extra cash. Wendy was trying to settle George down, as he was teething and probably had the loudest cry in the world. Being a 4-bedroom house, we were lucky as we were able to isolate the noise when I was doing the night shifts. How Wendy did this on such a regular basis I will never know, but she did, even depriving herself of sleep just to help the situation.

A few minutes before midnight, there was a loud knock at my door. To most people this might sound strange, but in my line of work there were sometimes occasions when we would oversleep, so one of us would go around and wake everyone else up – as we did not have mobile phones back then.

Wendy must have heard the knock, but knew I would answer it. She kept George in the other room, whilst listening to me get up. I staggered downstairs, not aware of the time, and certainly not expecting what I was opening the door to.

The stairs were split, and had a turn halfway down. Our front door was solid wood, with 4 small windows in an arc. The orange light from the streetlamps shone through the frosted glass at the top of the door, creating an eerie glow. At the bottom of the stairs I turned left. I reached out for the lock on the door, which was about shoulder height. It was a lock that you had to turn and pull, so using your right hand worked best. As I stood there, reaching towards the lock in my skimpy pants and my gold belcher chain around my neck, there was no thought of anything sinister.

I pulled the door towards me, and the orange light from the street flooded my hallway. When the door was three quarters of the way open, I found myself looking at 2 men. They were stood there, right in front of me, but even now in my memory they are just silhouettes. I still believe that by blocking this image, my subconscious is protecting me from the identity of the men.

The next few moments happened in slow motion. The guy to the right turned his head to look up the street, which I later discovered was to look at a third person, waiting on the other side of my next-door neighbour's house. I remember the silence. It was like someone had pressed mute on my ears. There were no voices, no sound, not even the engine noise of the waiting getaway car.

The same guy that had turned his head then nodded once in the same direction, and both men pushed forward. I held my hands up towards them in self-defence, with both my arms stretched out in front of me. Then the onslaught began. It felt as if there were more than 2 people, as they began to rain blows down on my head and my body. I wasn't aware that I was being stabbed, but my screams could be heard by Wendy upstairs, and by a passer-by who was walking his dog.

It was a frenzied attack, and with the weight of the blows I must have fallen to the ground. I may have been unconscious at some stage, as I do not remember going from a standing position to the foetal curl that I finished in. With my hands and arms over my head, I was trying to protect my skull from the beating, but not succeeding. I could feel my head being knocked from side to side, as they relentlessly pummelled me. The blades were penetrating my body all over. They repeatedly stabbed my left knee and thigh, and slashed at my torso with what I was later to discover was 2 blades placed in a Stanley Knife, separated with a wooden match. Apparently, this was almost impossible to stitch up afterwards.

I was not aware of what injuries I had at this stage, or what had caused them. I just remember what it felt like when they stopped. I went back to the silence. My memory still holds onto the image of their shoes and faces, blurry silhouettes, as if on a real-life news report. While I cannot remember their faces, I do know that they were both wearing blue jeans. One had a green bomber jacket on, a bit like an old skinhead Harrington jacket. One also had dark hair, possibly black. As soon as the assault stopped, they just turned and walked away slowly, still with no words or noise that I could hear.

For a brief moment, I just sat there, clutching my head – just making sure that they had gone. I do not remember any emotion at this stage. I just sat, motionless. I could not even feel the blood pouring from my wounds, and in some cases the blood was pumping out rather than pouring.

With blood gushing from my head, body and legs, I moved my right leg forward towards the door. I kicked it shut with the ball of my foot. This in itself was surprising, as the lock had been damaged when they entered. My falling body had smashed the door into the adjacent wall, denting the wall in the process.

It is really hard to describe how I began the crawl from the hallway towards the living room. I must have been aware of the injuries to my legs and arms, but still I began dragging myself across the floor. My hallway was only a couple of yards long, and I was possibly only half a yard away, but I recall that the feeling of entering the living room was like I had just arrived from a long journey.

I reached out and tried using the arms of the sofa as an aid to pull myself forward, blood pouring over whatever I touched. In the far corner of our living room I had a retro-looking cream coloured phone on a small corner shelf, which if standing was about waist high, but from my position it was above my head. I lifted the receiver and pushed the buttons 9....9....9. I screamed into the phone, "POLICE, AMBULANCE, FIRE, HELP! I've been beaten up!" My recollection of the conversation is vague, but I am sure I kept screaming for help, with the operator obviously trying to keep me calm to get the information she needed to send help.

The lady on the end of the phone did her job well. She got me calm, and managed to get a location from my jumbled mess of a story. I placed the handset back on the phone, and sat there to wait. I could now start to feel the pulse of the blood coming out of my body, especially from my head, which seemed to be flowing.

For some reason, I felt the urge to call my mum and dad, so reached out to grab the phone again. As I put the receiver to my ear, I heard the voice of the previous lady who had not disconnected from the line.

"I want to speak to my dad," I said.

The lady on the phone was very calm. She told me to put the phone down, count to 10, and then pick it back up and dial the number I wanted. How I did this I will never know, but I did. I counted to 10, then dialled my parents' number by pushing the little white buttons on the phone down.

"Dad, can you come around please? I have been beaten up." I wished that I had never made this call. Bringing my parents around to the aftermath and the scene they would have been confronted with, was an awful experience. I am sure that when you hear their own accounts of the evening, you will understand why that is one of my regrets.

CHAPTER 3

Bang, Bang, Bang

As I sat looking through my living room, completely ignoring the mess on the floor, I just focused on the door and the hallway – still lit by the orange light coming through the frosted glass windows at the top. Then, Wendy suddenly appeared at the living room entrance, holding George in her arms. She was quite clearly terrified, not knowing the carnage she was walking into, and her face told me how bad things were – it was a picture of complete and utter terror.

Blood was everywhere. It had splashed up the walls in the hallway, so high that it had gone over the height of the light switch. The blood on the wall by the light switch would have been Wendy's first view of what had happened. Fortunately, I do not think she noticed the pool of blood at the bottom of the stairs, or even the beginning of the trail that I had left behind. Wendy would also have had to step over an object at the bottom of the stairs, which belonged to my attackers.

Placing her first foot down in the hallway, still holding George in her arms, she immediately turned her head right in my direction, looking through the living room at me, still sat at the far end. I cannot imagine what was going through her mind at this stage, but her scream gave me an idea. As Wendy stepped cautiously forward, I could see her looking to her right, staring at the blood on the arm and cushion of the sofa. She took another step towards me, turning her head to the left, looking at our other sofa, also now splattered with my blood. I could feel her fear. Another scream was muffled but continuous as she progressed towards me. The carpet was saturated from where I had crawled through the living room, which meant that Wendy was walking through my blood.

Quite clearly not knowing what to do, Wendy walked slowly past me into the kitchen and grabbed a tea towel, which she then brought to me. As I reached out to take the tea towel from her shaking hand, I could only feel sorrow. I must have had the look of a man who was about to die. George was just looking at me, not knowing what this was all about. He was only a year old, so who knows what went on in his mind? I placed the tea towel to my head, but it came back soaked in red, so I just put it to one side and reverted back to placing my hands over the top of my eyes to try and stop the blood blocking my sight.

I am not sure if we spoke at this point, or any point for ages. Wendy just sat down on the edge of the blood-splattered sofa, with George still in her arms. It is strange to think that even in this horrendous moment there was a time to smile. George, sitting on Wendy's lap, on the only dry spot on our sofa, saw me placing my hands over my eyes and moving them away every couple of seconds. He thought I was playing "peek a boo" and laughed at me because of this. Innocence is a wonderful thing, but as I will reveal later in the book, this moment had a bigger impact on George than we could have imagined.

As I sat on the living room floor, I started to become cold. It was gradual at first, but then it sharpened, and I started to shiver. The blood had run down from my body, my pants were soaked with blood, and at this moment in time I felt like I was sitting in a flood. To me, the blood was 6 inches deep. Obviously this was not the case, but that's how it felt. I can remember the cold so vividly. It was a cold like I have never felt before, and have never had since.

Because of my complaints about how cold I was, Wendy decided to go back upstairs to get me a cover. She recalls how she deliberated over which cover to give me, as she did not want blood all over our favourite quilt cover. The mind works in strange ways in times of shock. Eventually Wendy returned back to the room, and covered my bloodied body, which was still pumping out blood from all the puncture wounds. One in particular, on my back, was big enough to put your whole hand in.

As we sat looking at each other, both in a state of shock, there was a banging at the door which startled both of us. They were calling us by name, so quite clearly it was not my attackers, but Wendy just screamed at them to go away. The knocking stopped, and once again the room fell silent. We were later to find out that the eldest daughter from next door and Keith from 2 doors down had heard the screams, and once they were convinced it was safe enough to venture over, they came to check on us.

I have never had an opportunity to say thank you to both of them for their kindness, so if you are reading this now then thank you. The neighbour from the other side had heard the commotion, but through fear and the desire to protect his family had decided not to venture out or investigate further, which I totally understand.

I am not sure how long it was before the police arrived, but they were pointed to our door by the two kind-hearted neighbours. All of a sudden, we heard this tremendous banging on the door, even louder than before – BANG, BANG, BANG! This was followed by a loud shout of "Police!" Wendy made her way to the front door, stopping a yard or so short, and somehow through shouting back at them managed to confirm that they were law enforcement. At this point I am not fully sure of how conscious I was, as the next moments are a bit of a blur, but Wendy's account later may shed some light on this.

Several police officers then came into our house. There were loads of questions, but I was asked repeatedly, "Who do you know in a red car, Darren?" "Who drives a red car, Darren?" The urgency in the officer's voice was quite apparent, but it was like I did not take onboard these questions. I just kept repeating that I didn't know. Obviously, I was a bit confused as to what a red car had to do with me sitting there bleeding to death.

I suppose at this stage I should have felt safe, but for some reason the actions of the police put me into a panic. There was nothing I could do other than just sit there looking at the pandemonium going on in my house, so I just sat there freezing. I was so, so cold. It is hard to describe what was going on in my mind at that moment, because I am not sure that I was fully with it, but the house was busy with people. The questions kept coming, the people just kept moving around me. It was almost like time had stood still for me, but had been sped up for everyone else.

The eyewitness who I mentioned earlier had called the police. He witnessed the 2 attackers leave my house and walk towards the lookout, who was waiting at the end of my road. They walked back to a waiting red car, which had the engine running, and a driver sitting ready for the getaway. The getaway car sped past the eyewitness whilst he was in the telephone kiosk speaking to the police, which was why the police were so interested in this red car that they had kept asking me about.

Suddenly, there was a bit of activity ahead of me – frantic voices at the open front door. The police had surrounded the house and alleyway outside with the POLICE DO NOT CROSS tape. By this point my mum and dad had arrived. As you can imagine, no plastic tape or police officer was going to stop them coming in.

So, back to why I wished I had never made the call to them. As they were trying to explain to the officers who they were, they were told by one officer, "We have done all we can for him." Essentially, the police at the scene thought that I was going to die. For a parent, this must have been devastating to hear. I had brought them into this situation, and I continue to wish that I had never done that.

I looked up and saw my mum and dad being ushered straight upstairs to Wendy and George, carefully stepping over a small cricket bat laying at the foot of the stairs. This was the second reason I wished I had not called them. The vision of me sat there being covered with a quilt, possibly on the edge of death, will stay with them forever. I can only imagine what they went through that night. Later in the book, they'll give their account of what they went through, but at the time of writing this chapter I had not read their accounts.

Eventually the ambulance turned up, and 2 paramedics came in. At first, they were pushed back, because a policeman had spotted a shiny object on the floor. This was the broken end of a Stanley blade, and they were not sure if this was evidence or had been walked in by the guys in green. Once again, my recollection of the moments following this are vague, but I can recall how my name was repeatedly used in every question, "Are you ok, Darren?" "Keep your eyes open, Darren" "Everything is going to be ok, Darren". Once again, 2 people who played a major role in saving my life – the paramedics – are people whom I will never see again, and will never have the opportunity to truly thank. I believe that their calming influence worked wonders in keeping me alive.

The paramedics began to address my wounds, wiping some of them clean before hurriedly covering them up with bandages. One wound in particular was down the front of my shin – this they just wrapped in bandage. The guys spent some time attending to the wound on my back, as it was quite clear that this was the one causing me the most issues.

The entire time that this was happening, I was motionless, completely unable to move unless being gently guided by the paramedics' hands. Then, it was time to move me. The 2 very caring helpers gripped hands, and picked me up in a cradle fashion, gently moving a metal tubular chair underneath my body. With great care, they placed some straps around me, and wrapped a red blanket around my shoulders. They began to move me slowly to the front door. With one of the guys pushing the chair from behind my head, and the other pulling the frame from my feet and walking backwards, I passed the bottom of my stairs. I finally got to see, close up, what I thought was one of the weapons used on me.

The whole time I had been sat there, I was looking towards my front door, at an object at the bottom of the stairs. Initially, I would have described this as a small cricket bat, but as I came closer I realised that it was in fact a meat cleaver, wrapped in cardboard and cling film as a holster. At this moment, the realisation hit me...

"I'VE BEEN STABBED!" I screamed. "I'VE BEEN FUCKING STABBED!"

The paramedics immediately stopped what they were doing, and started trying to calm me down, before progressing forward. In the writing of this book, I have had to dig deep. I have had to find my way back into memories that I had long since buried, and the recollection of that moment, realising that I had been stabbed, still moves me to tears.

As the paramedics wheeled me to the waiting ambulance, I can remember very clearly that an apparent air of calmness overcame me. This moment is what the cover of the book describes. I looked up at the beautifully clear October night sky, a view that for some reason still makes me smile, even now over 20 years later.

There were so many stars, and so bright. The sky was an incredible bluey black, but crisp in colour. This was a strange moment, which seemed to last for ages, but the reality was that it probably only lasted for a few moments, until the paramedics got me into the ambulance. Why I remember this so well, I do not know, but I think that it might be because this was the time – in my mind at least – that it seemed as if it was all over. Even now, whenever I look up at the stars on a clear evening, that moment comes back to me.

After what seemed like an age, the paramedics wheeled me into the ambulance. A policewoman climbed into the back, along with Wendy. The doors slammed shut, and everything went black.

CHAPTER 4

Red and Blue

I am told by Wendy that during the trip to the hospital, I kept asking if we could have the sirens on, as I had never been in an ambulance before. My persistence forced the driver to shout back, "Tell him we have just gone through a red light, that might keep him quiet!" I am also told that there were not enough seats in the ambulance, so I offered my lap as a place for the policewoman. She did not take up the offer. Even in my worst moments, I was trying to put a smile on people's faces!

I don't know how near I came to death that night, but I am sure it was close. I vaguely recall the reaction of the staff upon my arrival – abject horror – although once again I may have slipped in and out of consciousness, and my memories are extremely hazy. I had often watched TV dramas such as *Casualty* and *Holby City*, but now I was featuring in my very own episode. The journey through the hospital corridors was just like being in a TV show, with the lights on the ceiling flashing past me as we rushed past those cold looking walls.

I ended up in a large room, with a nurse and Wendy by my side. My head was being held over what I can only describe as a trough, and a small shower was being used to clean me, because the blood had started to congeal in my hair and was preventing them from stitching me up.

These moments are all a bit messy in my head, as I cannot seem to place them in the order that they happened. Whenever I recollect things, they change, so I will just say what I think happened. The hospital staff started by dealing with the gaping wound in my back, as this was the biggest of all the wounds. I was told that they were going to sew inside the hole, as just sewing the outside would not work, due to the sheer size of the wound.

There was a funny moment during this episode. As the nurse slowly removed a bandage which had been placed around my right shin, down the front of the shin was what at first looked like a very long gash. The blood had dried, but as they went to wipe the wound clean, the blood just wiped away with no wound underneath at all. In their urgency to get me to the hospital, the paramedics had just bandaged everything that looked like a wound. I am sure they would have been ribbed about that if their colleagues had found out.

With the bulk of the openings in my skull, there was quite a bit of time spent on this. To help with the pain of the stitches going in, they were injecting me using a hypodermic needle – with a chemical that was supposed to numb the pain. Unfortunately, it was excruciatingly painful every time the needle went in, so I asked if they could just sew with no injection. I can remember the feeling of them pulling at the skin on my head as they pulled the cotton through, and then tied off each section. I was told by the nurse that she had stopped counting the stitches at around 40, but there were not too many more after that.

At some point Wendy was taken away by the police to answer some questions. I wouldn't see her again until I got out of hospital. I just remained with this nurse talking to me about all sorts of things, which must have kept me calm. The nurse was telling me about the CICB, which stands for Criminal Injuries Compensation Board. This was a government body set up for people like me. Although it was something that I had never heard of before, this information became very useful at a later date.

Following this, I was then moved to a room within the main hospital, in or near A&E. My dad was with me at this point, along with an armed police officer who was there to protect me from anyone coming back and trying to finish what they had started. After several examinations, a doctor explained to my dad that there was some concern over one of my pupils either dilating or not dilating, I am not sure which, but he believed that this could have been caused by blood getting onto the back of my eyeball.

I am not sure how long we spent in this room, or how I was moved, but I ended up in a small ward on a bed with no one around me. Where everyone had gone I do not know, but I just laid there, looking at the glass doors. Then, all of a sudden, several police officers and nurses burst into the room. They surrounded me and dragged me over to another bed, in another area within the hospital.

Apparently, a man had been spotted wandering the hospital grounds – and they believed he was looking for me. This later proved not to be the case, but as you can imagine this was not an everyday incident, so the whole hospital was on high alert.

Following this, now in my new bed, I finally managed to settle down and get some sleep. I can comfortably say that this constituted the worst night of my life!

I woke up to sunlight coming through the small windows at the top of my bed. In my ward there were 4 other beds, all with elderly ladies in them, and a small podium where a staff nurse or sister stood.

As I lay there looking at the nurse, a young man came in. He was wearing a white shirt, black tie and black trousers, and carrying a metal briefcase. This made me really nervous. My body tensed, and I began to shake again. I heard him tell the nurse that he was here to change the toner in her fax machine, to which she replied, "We do not have a fax machine in here." As you can imagine, to me this was someone coming to finish the job, but the man just apologised and left the room.

This left me shaken and on edge. Not long after the young man had left, an older guy approached the nurse and spoke very quietly to her. Then, turning to point in my direction, he began to walk towards me. Now, I am not a movie buff, but this was like being part of a Bond film! The guy was wearing what looked like a brand new blue boiler suit, with perfectly polished black shoes. As he came closer I observed his name badge, which said *Jim Reeves*. Now the younger ones reading this may have never heard of Jim Reeves, but the older folks amongst you might know that Jim Reeves was the name of a famous wartime singer. Naturally, I jumped to the conclusion that this was a made-up name, and the older guy was a hitman who had come to finish me off!

As he got closer, I started to panic. I jerked my body hard to the side, and threw myself off the bed. I landed hard on the floor. I didn't see the man's reaction, but he turned very quickly, and left the ward. It later emerged that this man was actually a genuine employee of the hospital – he was in fact the maintenance guy. What I had not realised was that the news of my arrival had circulated around the hospital, and everyone wanted to come and see the big news story in person. This incident still brings a smile to my face today, although it gave me a huge fright at the time!

Later on during the day, my brother-in-law – Smithy – turned up to bring me home.

I could not have wished for a better person to take this responsibility, Smithy was brilliant. As you can imagine, I was sore, my body ached and my head was all over the place, and even then I was still not fully aware of how many injuries I had.

Getting out of the bed and into the clothes that Smithy had brought along was less than easy. I slowly pulled myself to the edge of the bed and dropped my feet to the floor. The whole time I could feel the tightness on my skin from wounds and stitches, but Smithy was extremely patient and caring, and he didn't make too much of a fuss over me. Thank you Smithy, this was a great help.

To go through what I had endured the previous night, only to be walking out of the hospital the following day, was nothing short of a miracle to me. These days, I think things would have been very different, and I'd have had a longer stay in the hospital.

However, I was not to know that this was just the beginning of a very long road to recovery. My first steps out of the hospital were only the start.

CHAPTER 5

Home

Smithy drove me to my mum and dad's house in Potter Street, Harlow. This was a strange experience, because there was a large part of me that was still unaware of my surroundings or what was going on. As you can imagine, my mum wanted to care for me, my dad wanted to kill someone, and Wendy was still in shock. Everyone had their opinion on what we should do, and in our own way we were all still trying to come to terms with what had happened.

There was a constant stream of visitors to the house, some who just wanted to be nosy, some to make sure I was genuinely alright, and some that probably felt they needed to say they'd done their bit. Wendy's brother Tony turned up, and as he was leaving decided to do his "big brother" bit, by poking me in the chest and telling me that I had better look after his sister. I suppose people deal with things in different ways, and he was just being protective of his little sister.

In an unusual turn of events, my friend Harvey also knocked at the door, with Dan in tow. While this may not seem strange, remember that this was 1996. We didn't have access to mobile phones back then like we do now, so it was hard to imagine how he would have heard so soon after the event.

Obviously, given what had happened, my mind was very much on edge. Harvey's visit made me feel a little suspicious, as if he knew something more about what had happened to me. I cannot remember my actual conversation with Harvey about this, but I do know that my dad told both Dan and Harvey, in no uncertain terms, that if this had anything to do with them at all then he would kill them. Some may say that this was just an "angry dad" statement but I am sure that if our thoughts were anywhere near accurate, then my dad's reaction would have been fairly volcanic.

At some point that evening we must have eaten, and I am sure there were more visitors than I have mentioned. My memory is sketchy, but I do remember our friend Debbie McGhee coming around to see us. This was nice, as it gave Wendy someone to talk to, and even confide in if it was needed. Debbie was possibly our closest friend, and still is today, as she has lived nearly every minute of our lives with us along with Stuart and Rachel.

After such an eventful 24 hours, my mum and dad eventually went to bed. I had managed to fall asleep on the living room floor, whilst Wendy and Debbie sat talking. After some deliberation, Wendy and Debbie decided to wake me, to try and encourage me to go to bed too. Naturally, it was not an easy thing to do, but almost to the minute at midnight, just 24 hours after the attack, I awoke suddenly – a little bit startled, but ok all things considering. Midnight was always going to prove to be a significant time in my life going forward.

The next few days were mostly spent with the police coming around to my mum and dad's house, asking a million and one questions about all sorts of things. Could I describe the attackers' faces? What were they wearing? Did I know anyone who had a grudge against me? Did I see the getaway car? They were convinced that the attackers had used a Ford XR2, which was a popular sporty little car back then.

The only connection that I had to a small red sports car, was from about a week or so before the attack. I was out in the early hours, delivering newspapers to the newsagents as usual. I pulled around to a parade of shops in Bishops Stortford, called Heath Row. Outside the shops there was a very large pavement area, with car parking spaces in front of this.

As I drove closer to the shop, I pulled up on the pavement, next to a red Renault 5. As I bumped up the kerb next to the Renault, I spotted 2 guys sitting in the front of the car, which made me a little concerned as to what they were up to. If it had been me sitting in that car, and a large white van drove up close and then bumped up the pavement next to me, I would have turned my head and looked around, but not these 2 guys. They just stayed looking forward, and didn't give so much as a glance in my direction.

Being a bit worried, I parked the van in a position where I could keep an eye on the car, whilst I unloaded the papers into a metal box outside the shop. I finished my delivery, and then quite slowly pulled the van down the other side of the Renault, once again bumping the kerb. Again, they didn't look at me, not even once, which bothered me a bit. Fortunately, as I carried on with my round I spotted a police car. I flagged it down and reported the situation to the officer inside.

For some time during the investigation into my attack, this was quite a focus, as it seemed too much of a coincidence. However, the police officer to whom I had reported this was away on holiday at the time of the attack. Once my investigating officer had found him, he informed us that he had very little to say. He went on to investigate the car and the men sitting inside, but they had told him they were just waiting for their friend. The officer said he informed them that they could not wait here, so they just moved on without the alleged friend they were waiting for. He hadn't taken any names or any registration details, so this ended up drawing a blank. This did not seem right to me, so I spent an awful lot of time trying to remember the faces from that car, in the hope that it would bring back the faces from the attack, but no luck.

Whilst in hospital there had been a mention of an organisation called Victim Support. At the time I had never heard of this organisation before, but then during one of the police interviews they were mentioned again, and it was suggested that they could call me – to which I agreed.

Throughout the early days of my recovery, there were quite a few people who were extremely helpful. In particular, I would like to thank Detective Constable Mick Clarke. It was Mick who gave me his phone number to contact him on, at any time of day or night, which is something that I took advantage of on the first night we returned to 101 Brockles Mead.

During our stay at my mum and dad's house, we had decided that leaving our own home empty for any length of time, in an area less than perfect, may result in a break-in. Most people in the area would have heard what had happened, leaving an opportunity for thieves to come in and help themselves. With this in mind, we went around to empty the house of a few of our more personal things. It is sad to think that this was in our thoughts, given the events that had taken place, but it was how the situation and area made us feel.

When it came to moving our things, my dad recruited the help of his boss, Peter Wiggins. Along with Smithy, the 3 of them went in first. I followed with my mum and mother-in-law in a second car. As we parked, I made a comment that I think hurt my mum, without meaning to obviously. Trying to be practical, I said, "When we get to the house I may get a bit emotional, but I don't want any cuddly stuff please!" As you'll know, all a mum wants to do is cuddle their child when they cry or are in pain. I did not get the cuddle, nor did I fall apart into a snivelling wreck, but I will never forget the feeling of anger that came over me as I started to walk through the scene for the first time.

The blood was everywhere. It was all over the carpets, the sofas and the telephone. The smell of the blood was overwhelming. I just wandered around aimlessly, looking in shock at the state of my once lovely home. This was another moment where the detail is still vague, but the smell for some reason will stay with me forever. I think that there was a sense of shock and disbelief on everyone's face. Along with me, they all took a few moments to comprehend what they were looking at.

Peter Wiggins is a great man, and in those days was still a very hard man (following years of studying martial arts and an upbringing that had taught him to be tough) but he was moved by the scene – which took me by surprise. Then the moment came. It was time to get practical, so we all kicked into tidy-up mode. Well, when I say all, I mean everyone except me. I just wandered around in a daze, collating my thoughts and trying to put this all together.

At some point, I went outside and stood just looking up the street, when Smithy came out to check on me. As we stood talking, a local group of lads well known in the area for all the wrong reasons were gathering and looking in our direction. They then started to walk towards myself and Smithy, putting us on edge for a moment. However, they turned about 20 yards short of where we were standing. I later heard that what had happened to me was quite big news in certain circles. They did not know me, so they had decided that I was someone to befriend and keep an eye on, inadvertently ensuring that my home was now safe from scumbags. Obviously I was not aware of this at the time, and I was still on edge, so it made me nervous for a while.

We cleared our important things, and then went back to my mum and dad's house, where we were to stay for some months. Although this was brilliant for us, we knew it would not be forever, and at some point we needed to move back into our home and begin the process of getting back to normal...well, as normal as possible.

Earlier in this book, I said that I had 2 major regrets over the events following the stabbing. The first was calling my mum and dad after the attack, and the second was as follows. Whilst living at my parents' house, I fancied popping out for a couple of pints one Sunday afternoon, but Wendy was saying that we had no money. My mum and dad were trying to help, by saying they had beer in the fridge. It was at this point that I announced to them all, "I wish I was dead". Quite clearly this was an overreaction to the situation, but it was actually the first sign of clinical depression – which I would later be diagnosed with by my NHS counsellor.

I have never ever spoken to my mum about this statement, but I am sure those words hurt her so much, and for that I am truly sorry. It is also important to point out that as sorry as I was for saying that, in my mind I meant it, which was clearly not a good thing at all.

With my mood and my mental state becoming increasingly unpredictable, Wendy decided that getting me back home would be the best thing for us. My doctor at the time, Dr Richards, also agreed with this. He suggested that as I was a lifelong hard worker, it would also help with my recovery if I made steps towards getting back to work. At the time, I put several obstacles in the way of that idea, but he was right.

So, soon enough, we moved back to 101 Brockles Mead. The day we moved back was strange, for a number of reasons. Earlier in the book I told you that the impact on our 1-year old George was far greater than we had expected. Well, as we walked him from the car to the house for the first time, he fell to the ground, about 5 yards away from the front door. He clearly did not want to go any closer, and the fear was evident on his face. This was really hard to deal with, but we picked George up and made our way into the house.

After we'd settled back in as best as we could, we decided to go to bed as early as possible. I had been told that going to bed when not tired would help me to relax and sleep better. I was not to know that at exactly midnight, the phone next to our bed would ring. Nervously I answered the call, but there was just silence from the other end. I immediately put the phone back down and rang Detective Constable Mick Clark.

Somehow, they traced the number of the caller, and within minutes the police were on their way to the address where the number was located. Unfortunately for some poor guy working at United Glass that night, his little secret was uncovered. It turns out the guy had been having some extra marital activity during his nightshift, popping out from work to his lover's house, but would call using the office phone to check the coast was clear. So, when he heard a man's voice answer the call, he just hung up.

I'm not sure how he explained that one to his workmates and wife. The good news for Wendy and I was that the call was completely unrelated to the attack, he had just dialled the wrong number, so we were able to relax and sleep a bit better the following evening.

As I was now getting back into what was called normal life, we decided to go to a local party. This was being held in the function hall of The Maypole, a social club that I had used back when I was in school, and a place where everyone knew everyone. In the past, I had spent many, many hours in there, drinking with the club community. This was a safe place to be, where I could relax and be myself, and within a short space of time I was having a laugh and enjoying myself.

One of my friends – Jim, who I had not seen since the attack, had approached me to see how I was. This was a big thing to Jim, as he was a shy guy, very pleasant, but often unsure what to say. Jim just asked me how things were, to which I answered, "I am ok, Jim. I just have to watch myself with the booze."

Jim, now feeling a little more confident, asked, "Is that because you are still on medication?"

"No," I replied. "It's because it pours all over the floor", signalling with my hands the pouring action out of my body.

Jim just stood there, whilst several of us laughed. He did not know how to take it. I am sorry Jim for not taking that moment as seriously as you did, but you did make me realise that there were times when I needed to keep my sense of humour to myself. This was really impacting on people in different ways, and not everyone would be able to handle it with a giggle. There were many moments where I would meet people for the first time after the attack, and because Jim had taught me a lesson, I managed to decide who to mock the moment with, or when it was better to be serious.

For example, me and Stuart Beck had decided that it would be funny to paint the white outline of a body on the floor, around where my blood had stained the concrete in the house. We thought we could make it like a scene from *Police Academy* or *Naked Gun*, so eventually when the carpet was renewed by someone in the future it would give them the fright of their lives. Luckily for us we had Wendy and Rachel putting the needle back on our moral compass, so we never went through with it. Looking back, I am glad, because there were 2 people who would have been very upset with us mocking such a serious situation.

Earlier on in this book, I mentioned that I had worked with a guy called Vic. Now Vic was a character to say the least, and whilst we were working delivering the papers we had become friends. Vic had decided to get married, and thought that I would be a great person to look after his business whilst he was away on honeymoon. Vic was on his honeymoon whilst the stabbing took place. Although I didn't mind running his business for him, what I didn`t know was that Vic had been involved with some really seedy people. So, upon Vic`s return from honeymoon, people started to point the finger at him, saying that the attack was meant for him and that he should be very afraid.

Now, Vic was a pretty tough guy, but not in a world where people could arrange a professional hit on him. So, after walking around at work and home looking like a scared man, he decided to hand himself in to the police. Strangely enough, this was a moment that makes me smile. When Vic was asked by the officers who might want to do this to him, he gave them a list as long as your arm! Once again this line of enquiry came to an abrupt end, but I decided to pay Vic a visit at work anyway, which gave him a bit of a fright. We spoke about what had happened and he could not have been anymore sorry than he was. He really was still convinced that he was next, and not long after that he moved away from the area. Wherever you are Vic, I hope you are safe and well.

CHAPTER 6

Kilroy

During the first few weeks after the attack, it's fair to say that I was a little blind to the impact that the event was having on those around me. For example, my sister Teresa was emotionally distraught, and she had been severely affected by what had happened. Looking back, I am not sure who noticed her grief, but it certainly wasn't me. Despite this, Teresa still went about trying to help me. She wanted to let the whole world know that her big brother had been stabbed. She wanted me to get some sort of recognition for this, or acknowledgement, but in her own way she was also trying to cover up her own pain, by telling others about what had happened.

Unbeknownst to me, Teresa had spoken to a television production company, who produced a TV programme called *Kilroy*. Back in the day, *Kilroy* was a famous daytime chat show, and a must-see for anyone who was at home midweek. The show was hosted by the broadcaster and politician, Robert Kilroy-Silk, and at this time had been running for 10 years, so everyone knew about it.

Teresa had called me to say that I may get a call from someone on the production team, and that they were going to ask me a few questions about my attack, to see if they could fit my story into one of their programmes. Almost immediately a very nice lady called, and asked me about my attack. Now, I need to point out at this stage that the attack happened at midnight on the 7th October. I spoke to the lady from the show on the 25th October, just 18 days after I'd been stabbed, so it's fair to say that I was not of sound mind at this stage. Nevertheless, I agreed that I would appear on the show on my birthday, 28th October.

On the day in question, the lady that rang me had arranged for a car to come to Harlow, pick us all up, and drive us to the studios in Teddington. As I had never been on a TV show before, the day was something I will always remember, even down to the dilemma in our house as to what we should wear. Ultimately, we kept it neutral. I went with a grey shirt, and Wendy wore a white blouse.

Upon arrival, we were looked after very well, and led to what is commonly known as a green room. This is where all the people who were going to appear on the show, or take part in some form, met up for a chat and a cup of tea. At this stage, all I knew was that the show was going to be about knife crime in the UK, and my story was just one example of a crime involving knives.

The green room was a strange place, as it was all so bright and warm with very few staff about, and just a self-service coffee and tea area. This is where I met a very nice man, who had been stabbed whilst trying to protect his shop from being burgled. It was at this point that I realised that I was suddenly not alone, in my world of being a victim of knife crime. The room was full of people who had a story to tell, some of whom were there because they had lost someone to knife crime. I found this incredible. I couldn't believe that we could fill an entire room with victims of knife crime, and I started to wonder how many other victims were out there. After all, this was just one room, a small snapshot of public life.

Whilst finishing off our tea and biscuits, a member of the *Kilroy* team came in and announced that we were all to follow them to the studio. At this point, Wendy handed George over to a nurse, who placed

George in a crèche whilst we attended the show. George was what you might call a very clingy baby. He would cry continually if he was not sure of his environment, but the lovely lady took George – confident that she would win him over, and told us that we should get on our way and not worry.

So, off we went, following the crew member through the labyrinth of equipment and corridors with all the walls painted in a matt black. As we entered the studio I suddenly started to feel very nervous, and Wendy was very much feeling the same. I'm sure that if I had asked her at the time, she would have told me that she'd rather have been anywhere else than there, but as always she was by my side for support.

The studio was much smaller than I was expecting, but once inside it was exactly what I had seen on the TV. The seating was set out in stadium fashion, almost circular, going around the studio with 2 walkways separating the rows of seats. This was to allow Kilroy himself to get between the guests and speak to them, and give them the chance to put across what they wanted to say.

When we entered the studio, and saw the seating for the first time, there were already some people seated. I was later to find out that these were young men who carry knives for various reasons, who were there to put their case across that knife crime was just part of normal life. These people were not in the green room with us beforehand. I would say that there were about 60 or 70 people in the studio once we were all seated, with a mix of young and old, as well as male and female. There were also a few people in suits, who were officials and MPs from various areas. I was placed about 4 rows from the front, but by the aisle, so that Kilroy could sit next to me when he was ready.

So, we got underway. The show's theme tune started, and the camera focused on the huge neon lit KILROY letters at the back of our seating, with the "I" in *Kilroy* being replaced with an exclamation mark. Kilroy himself was stood directly next to me, prior to walking down the steps to begin his introduction. He walked to the centre of the studio in front of us, just as the lights came up, and stood in the centre of the stage. In his hand, he was holding a vicious looking knife. Turning to the camera, he informed the audience that knives like this were readily available in our shops, and online via mail order. He then asked the following question:

"Why would anyone want to buy or own a knife, like this one?"

Following this, Kilroy turned and took a seat. He introduced a young man called Jason, who explained that he carried a knife regularly, and admitted to using the knife on several occasions. Jason was a tough looking character, and to be fair to him he conducted himself very well, especially as the bulk of the audience wanted to see him struggle.

He told us all that he carried a "sheath knife" in a holster, for protection. Then, it was the audience's turn to respond to this. A lady spoke up against Jason, informing him that her son had been stabbed in a supermarket whilst protecting a young woman, following a shoplifting incident. Jason defended himself well on this one. He clearly believed that what he was doing, and how he lived, was right for him. Meanwhile, I sat listening to Jason speak, my face a picture of anger and borderline rage. I simply couldn't come to terms with what he was saying.

Next, the conversation turned a bit, as Kilroy took his place on the stairs next to me. He placed his microphone in front of a lady to my left, on the opposite side of the stairway, called Lyn Costello. Lyn was representing an organisation called "MAMaas" which stands for "Mums Against Murder and Aggression". Lyn`s story was about her husband, who was stabbed after an altercation outside a pub. Although Lyn's husband survived, his friend (who was also stabbed) died from the attack. Lyn was clearly a passionate lady when it came to this subject, and really took young Jason to task. However, Jason stood up for himself. They both argued the case about knives, and Lyn was having none of Jason`s 'woe is me, I live on a council estate' agenda. Lyn also came from a council estate, and had brought up her children on that estate.

Sitting there listening to them argue, I was just getting angrier and angrier. I can't imagine what I looked like, but inside I was absolutely livid. Finally, I could no longer contain myself. Pointing my finger at Jason, I began:

"I come from one of your council estates, mate. I got a knock on the door at midnight, and a bloke like you…"

Jason interrupted me, "You can`t say a bloke like me, you don`t know me!"

"You carry a knife!"

We both repeated our statements. With anger bubbling inside of me, and my voice clearly changing due to the rage, I finished with, "You carry a knife, that makes you as low as him, the bloke that done me." Watching this back, there were certain things that I said that sound silly now, but at the time passions were running high, and I was clearly still in shock at what I had been through.

Following this discussion, Kilroy encouraged me to tell the audience about what happened to me. Keeping it very brief, I described what I had been through, but finished it off with, "That was over 3 weeks ago now!" Watching it back, that now seems crazy. 3 weeks after the most horrendous event of my life, there I was, arguing with a young scouse lad on national TV.

Kilroy asked me how I felt, to which I replied with, "Words can`t describe how I feel. I want to see the bloke that done me with a knife in his back, going through what I had gone through!"

Jason came back at me with, "You are saying exactly what I said."

"I don't carry a knife. I should be able to leave my house and not worry about carrying a knife." At this point, the tension was building, and if I was being honest the TV show had now disappeared from my mind. I wanted this conversation with Jason, and I possibly even wanted this chat away from cameras. Kilroy then placed the microphone back in front of Lyn, who was itching to defend me – "He wouldn't actually put the knife in someone`s back!" She then explained how we all say things in anger, but the reality is they are just words for the majority of people.

Kilroy then moved the conversation to the guy sitting directly in front of me. Dressed in his Adidas tracksuit top and baseball cap, he turned back to face me. "If you had a knife, and you was attacked by someone with a knife, you would use the knife!"

With my temper now coming to the surface, I responded with, "I don't carry a knife, mate. I don't carry a knife."

At this point, you can see how if this conversation had been held anywhere other than a TV studio, then it could have got out of control. The guy replied to me, saying that if he broke into my house, and I had caught him in the kitchen, I would use whatever was at hand to defend myself or my property – possibly even a kitchen knife. I responded with, "Of course I would!" By this point, the guy was really bugging me. Unlike Jason, who I had a little bit of respect for, this guy seemed to be pushing all the wrong buttons.

Just off camera there was a young lad sitting next to Wendy, who felt it appropriate to contribute to this conversation away from the show's activities. This lad enraged me so much that I threw my right hand around in his direction and tried to grab his face. Unfortunately, I managed to clump the back of the heads of the people in front of me, and my elbow caught Wendy in the face. Kilroy had spotted this and kept his hand firmly on my left hand, forcing it down onto my knee. I am glad this part managed to get edited out before going to air, as I would have looked like a right idiot.

Kilroy interrupted the conversation, to allow the now visibly upset Wendy to say her piece. Her trembling voice and tears still anger and upset me so much, that when I watch this it brings me to tears again. I have decided that, once this book is finished, I will not watch the recording of that programme ever again. Seeing Wendy`s pain is just too much for me, and I have seen her go through too much pain over the years.

The conversation then moved on, with the bulk of the people in the studio turning on Jason, and even Kilroy was provoking Jason to see if he could get a reaction. Due to the nature of the programme there were all sorts of discussions from the people who had lost loved ones, to the legal aspects of knife attacks, and even a business owner who sells combat knives.

It has been really interesting watching the programme back, as it went backwards and forwards between various people – all with valid points, albeit some were more credible than others. Following the audience discussion, complete with various MPs and police officers having their say, the programme came to a close.

Because of the tension in the room, I was taken to one side and ushered very quickly through the black corridors, back to the green room, where the clearly stressed nursery nurse was clutching a screaming George.

Wendy took the tearful George from the lady, and we were asked to go and sign some forms. At this point I was given £40 for appearing on the show, and we were led very quickly to a waiting car outside the studio. This was all before the other attendees arrived back at the green room. I can still remember the anger inside me boiling up again as we left the car park, but I managed to contain it and just sat in silence for the journey home.

Talk Radio

Some months after my appearance on Kilroy, I was listening to a radio show whilst out in my car. The station was called *Talk Radio*, which at a later date was taken over and renamed to *Talk Sport*. As I listened, a show began which was going to talk about knife crime and the impact it has on society. I immediately pulled over by a petrol station, pulled out my phone, and dialled the show's contact number.

The show was hosted by a presenter called Mike Dickin, who had been a journalist for many years. On this day, Mike was joined by a celebrity doctor called Hilary Jones. I had seen Hilary Jones on several television shows, and heard him on many radio shows before that day. To be honest, when I called in and spoke to the researcher I was not expecting to be put through to the 2 presenters. After all, why would these very famous presenters want to know about my little story?

At first, I began to tell the story of my attack, and was asked several questions by both Mike Dickin and Hilary Jones. I really enjoyed this. However, I was not prepared for the general public to take such an interest in my story.

Mike stopped me at one point, so they could go to a break, but asked if I would stay on the line as someone had called in to speak to me when the show resumed. During the break, Hilary came on the phone to speak with me and explained that their switchboard had lit up with people from all over the country wanting to talk with me, and asked if I had time to answer all their questions. At last people were listening to my story, and the sympathy from callers was amazing. For a brief moment I completely forgot that I was being listened to by the nation, and just settled into this little moment of fame.

I have tried to get a recording from that day, but as of yet I have had no luck. Sadly, Mike Dickin was killed in a car crash near his home in Cornwall in 2006, but I will always have fond memories of my moment on the radio with him. This no-nonsense presenter, who had torn strips off many of his guests, just led me through the experience, sympathetically and amiably, and I will forever be grateful for that.

Kilroy, The second appearance

I am not sure where I was when I received the invitation to go back onto *Kilroy*, but when the lady on the phone told me that the programme was going to be about how we can solve violent crimes, I jumped at the opportunity. At the time, it had been two years since the attack.

The reason for the subject was down to the fact that a very famous TV presenter called Jill Dando had recently been murdered, and at the time the police thought this was down to a professional hit. The debate was going to be about violent crime, and what the police response should be. In my case, there were questions to be asked. Prior to getting on the show I was led to believe the show was going to be about professional hits that go wrong. So, once the show started, it was a little bit of a surprise to me.

With my previous visit to the studio, we had been picked up from our house and driven there and back, but on this occasion I went in my own car. However, the studio had laid out a parking space. It is so nice sometimes to just feel a little bit important, as I did upon my arrival.

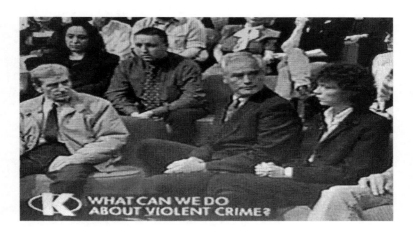

As before, we were invited to have a tea or coffee in the green room, where I was to meet several people who were due to share their stories on the show. One particular guy had spent over 2 years in prison, after cutting a guy that had come into his store to steal from him. It was a shame really, as this guy was used as a bit of a punchbag during the show, as people were saying that he was in the wrong for using a knife on the robber. For me personally, if the guy had not tried to steal then he would not have been stabbed, however that is a debate for another time.

Following the shopkeeper's story, Kilroy turned in my direction, with his microphone in hand. There was no "This is Darren" or any other prompt, I just began with my story. "People who do this sort of thing" was my first line. I followed this up with, "I was a victim of an attempted murder" and started to tell my story

Kilroy briefly interrupted me from time to time, asking questions, such as where I was stabbed and how many times. I described the wounds to him, keeping it brief, as I was in full flow. It is strange watching this back now. Compared to my first appearance, I was so much more composed, and I even articulated my point quite eloquently – which actually makes me feel quite proud of myself. Kilroy was excellent. He gave me all the time I needed to tell my story, which then gave the opportunity for me to talk about the impact that the attack had had on my mum and dad.

The conversation then moved onto the reaction by the police, and how I felt about their response. I explained to Kilroy that I was concerned that the police were pre-judgemental because of where I lived. Once again, Kilroy gave me all the time I needed to get my point across, but very cleverly moved the conversation to being about the police – which then brought in Detective Chief Superintendent Michael Burdis, who was Head of CID for South Yorkshire.

Superintendent Burdis spoke about how difficult the job of the police would be in these circumstances, which I agreed with. However, as soon as I had another opportunity, I brought up that after 4 days the police had come to me with no answers. They'd said it was just a case a of mistaken identity – tough luck basically. They also said that part of the problem with the investigation was that they couldn't find anyone who'd say a bad word about me. This prompted Kilroy to say, tongue in cheek, 'You must be a special person!' to which I responded with, 'They obviously didn't speak to my wife then!' This was a nice moment, because the whole studio audience were laughing at my response, which just made my confidence grow.

As we continued, a young lady that had lost her brother to knife crime wanted to support my point about the police arriving with an opinion before they begin their work. She also raised the issue that every time they tried to speak to the police for an update, they were told that it was 'privileged information'. This was something that I had spoken of when I was talking.

Michael Burdis was genuinely upset by the lady's story, and forthright in his condemnation of our investigating officers not coming to us before we went to them. This then sent the chat down a different direction, but I did get to have several opportunities to chip in with my opinions. It was also good to have Jenny Watson from Victim Support there as well, who wanted to bring to the programme what the role of Victim Support was.

I have gone through some strange emotions watching both the *Kilroy* episodes. After the first one, I made myself a promise never to watch the recordings ever again, but after watching the second episode I feel like I would watch it again – as I am so proud of how I came across and how I conducted myself. This feeling may be because I was there on my own, or possibly it's because this was 2 years after the attack. Whatever the reason, I am so pleased that I have experienced this and can now look back with fondness.

CHAPTER 7

Morley House

Although in this chapter I will discuss the fight for compensation, I could also have called the chapter "My Battle for Acknowledgement". You may remember me mentioning something called the Criminal Injuries Compensation Authority (CICA), earlier in the book. Well, ultimately, with no suspects and nobody to blame, I was left with no option but to use this organisation.

At first, it felt quite wrong to be talking about money after an incident like this. To be honest though, I needed something on which I could take out my anger. Once the initial fallout had passed, and with the investigation seemingly going nowhere, I needed something or someone to give acknowledgement that this was a really bad thing to happen to me.

I had already made the local newspaper, and taken part in a short interview on local radio 101.7FM, commonly known as Ten 17 (now Heart Radio). This was all done to try and help with the investigation, and was conducted under the guidance of the investigating officer Mick Clark, and the volunteers from Victim Support.

Despite this though, the only place where I could possibly receive real recognition was through the CICA. As you would expect, there were many forms that needed to be completed, and in my state of mind none were easy. I was asked to fill in the details of the attack, which was tough. I was also asked to complete forms on my earnings. As I was self-employed for times prior to the attack, this was also difficult to complete.

The CICA are now called the CICB, as they have changed the last word to Board. However, the CICA that I dealt with were set up by the government. According to their own website, they were responsible for 'dealing with compensation claims from people who have been physically or mentally injured because they were the blameless victim of a violent crime'. At the time, this was a lifeline to me. It seemed like I had found an organisation that would not only acknowledge what had happened, but also compensate me for my loss, both in my current earnings and any potential earnings that might be impacted by my mental state. Oh how wrong I was.

From the very beginning of the process, I was made to feel like I had done something wrong, as if it was my fault that I opened my door, and allowed those people to enter my home. Now, I am seriously hoping that the current regime at the CICA has changed over the past 21 years, but I can only write about my own experience. There were points following the attack which were just as bad as the stabbing itself, and this was one of them.

By November 1996 I had completed my first application for compensation, which had been sent to and acknowledged by the CICA. I then started to communicate with the CICA on the phone, trying to get into dialogue with them, and see where I was in the process. This was partly out of desperation for the money, but mostly I just wanted someone to put a huge arm around me and say that they were sorry for what had happened, and they were going to help me get through it.

In January 1997 I received a copy of a letter which had been sent by Yvonne Grant (Community Mental Health Specialist). In this letter, Yvonne had explained that I was originally referred to her by my doctor on 30th October 1996, suffering from depression and that I required urgent intervention by the CPN (not sure what that stands for). I'd been visiting Yvonne for some time by that point, and her assessment to the CICA was that my mental state during this time had ranged from that of a sense of deep loss, pessimism, rage, anger and hurt, to emotional pain, and that I was very tearful.

Yvonne also spoke about my ability to move back to my own home (from my parents' house), as at this stage this had not happened.

Even with this information, the compassion or understanding from the CICA was non-existent. I received more forms with an opening letter, stating that I must reply within 8 weeks of the date of the letter, as failure to do so would result in the application being refused under paragraph 13(c) of the scheme on the grounds of non-cooperation with the authority. It really felt like I was the criminal here, and my attempt to claim compensation was clearly not going to go through without a battle.

Then, at the end of February 1997, I received the following notification. Please look carefully at the letter, and try to imagine how you would feel. Imagine that you'd been physically and emotionally traumatised, violated, attacked in the comfort of your own home. Imagine reaching out desperately for someone to help you. Now, imagine being told that the mental anxiety this caused was worth a grand total of £50 – take it or leave it.

CRIMINAL INJURIES COMPENSATION AUTHORITY

CICA	Switchboard 0171 842 6800
Morley House	Direct dial 0171 842 6863
26-30 Holborn Viaduct	Fax 0171 436 0804
LONDON	Fax
EC1A 2JQ	DX

WEST ESSEX VSS	Your Ref 8527
KINGSMOOR HOUSE	
PARINGDON ROAD	Our Ref L/96/246587-CW0C
HARLOW	
ESSEX	Date 26/02/1997
CM19 4QT	

Dear Sir/Madam,

REGARDING: DARREN BARDEN

INCIDENT DATE : ON 08/10/1996

NOTIFICATION OF FINAL AWARD

Having considered your application for compensation, I have determined that you are entitled to a sum of **£2675.00**

This sum has been calculated as follows:

AWARD FOR INJURY UNDER THE TARIFF SCHEME

Injury Description	Band	Amount		
SIGNIFICANT SCARRING TO TORSO	6	£ 2500.00	100%= £	2500.00
MINOR SCARRING TO LEG(S)	2	£ 1250.00	10%= £	125.00
TEMPORARY MENTAL ANXIETY	1	£ 1000.00	5%= £	50.00
		Total injury award :	£	2675.00

DEDUCTION OF MONIES ALREADY RECEIVED

An interim award has already been paid so this will be deducted, the amount of this deduction is :   £   0.00

Therefore the total amount payable by us is: £   2675.00

If you decide to accept this decision you should complete the enclosed acceptance form and return it without delay. You do not become entitled to be paid any money until we have received notification in writing that you accept our decision. However, paragraph 58 of the scheme, states that if an applicant disagrees with the decision of the authority, the applicant may apply to have

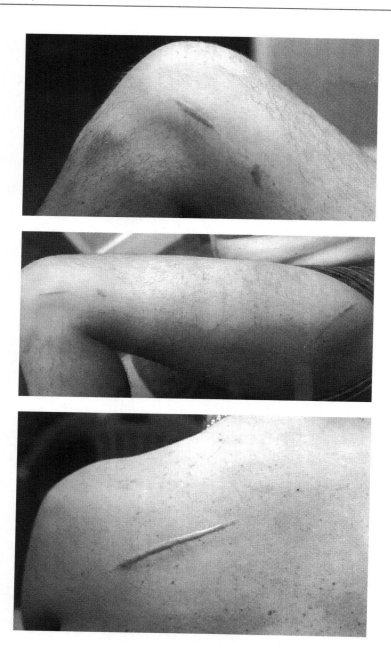

If you look closely at the form, you'll also see that they very generously assumed my mental anxiety was 'temporary'. I wonder if they thought I would be better in 28 weeks? This is what is stated in their information about the grades of compensation. Although this book is titled *Let's Skip To The Good Bits* I'm sure you can appreciate by now that recovering from this incident wasn't quite that simple. Naturally, I was pretty offended by this. It felt like they were just telling me to go away, as if I wasn't worthy of real compensation, or that my suffering wasn't significant.

As a result of this, I made the decision to have my application reviewed by the authority. This antagonised the CICA quite considerably. At this stage, we were coming to the end of May 1997, and the money I had borrowed from various people was starting to become a burden to me. I needed, and wanted, to repay those who had helped me. Thus, I was informed that I could make an application for an interim payment. This was successful, and I was eventually given £2,000, providing I completed more forms.

It was at this stage that I decided to try and claim for my loss of earnings, but once again I was met with "the CICA can only consider applications for loss of earnings if the applicant is likely to lose earnings or earning capacity for longer than 28 weeks".

I still have all the correspondence between myself and the CICA, which makes for interesting reading when trying to reflect on the situation for this book. Eventually I received news in November 1997 over a year after the attack, confirming that after careful consideration under paragraph 59 of the 1996 scheme, I would be awarded £7,500 – of which I had already received an interim payment of £2,000. So, after a yearlong battle, a further £5,500 was sent out to me.

When I heard this, I was devastated. I can remember sitting on the floor of my kitchen, crying my eyes out whilst reading this letter. Eventually I composed myself and made my way to the offices of

Victim Support, where the incredible Ronni Ayers once again clicked into action and made me aware that there was another stage we could take my claim to – the appeal stage.

So, once again we began to complete more forms. Eventually a date was set for me to attend a hearing in front of the appeal panel: Friday 12th June 1998 at 10.15am, within the offices of the CICA Appeals Panel at 26-30 Holborn Viaduct, London. EC1A.

Prior to attending, I was given a series of instructions by the appeal panel. These instructions made me feel like a criminal, as if I'd done something wrong and was now being judged. I was asked to read the "preliminary bundle" of documents and ensure that all was correct. I was also asked to make sure that I had these with me at the oral hearing. Along with this, I was sent a checklist, and had to ensure that the bundle had all medical reports from doctors, psychiatrist and consultants. Finally, I was told to make sure that all the evidence was correct, or consequences would follow.

When Friday 12th June arrived, Wendy, our friend Debbie, and I all made our way to London for the hearing. Debbie had come along to look after Shannon – our second child, who was born in 1998.

We were greeted by a very nice man, who was to be my presenting officer – Mr Millett. The first thing he did was to try and prepare us for the hearing. The building was a fantastic place, modern, and built in an area of London that was steeped in history, but it was hard for us to appreciate this. On that day, it just felt cold and intimidating.

Prior to entering the hearing room, Wendy was informed that she was only allowed in as support, and any comments from her would mean they would have her removed from the hearing! So warm and welcoming to a woman who had been there every step of the way, who was just as much a victim of this crime as me...

The hearing room was about the size of a small hall. There was a line of tables running away from us along the left-hand wall, and coming off those tables were several more running along the far wall. We were pointed towards a lone table situated almost centrally in the room. It reminded me of a school exam desk – wooden top, four thin metal legs, with two grey plastic chairs placed facing all the other tables. It was as if everything had been set up to make us feel uncomfortable and alone.

We sat down on the plastic chairs, and the meeting began. The first two people sitting to my left were representatives from the CICA. They were there to make notes on the day's events, and to my knowledge did not contribute in any way. At the third table to my left was the presenting officer Mr Millett. He was a very pleasant guy, who seemed to be the only person with any compassion for my situation.

Seated at the far tables were Rt. Hon. Eric Stockdale, a judge, then to his right as I looked at them was Ms. Geraldine Linley, a barrister, and finally the furthest person to my right was Dr Pinto, who I believe was a psychiatrist, but was only introduced as a medical representative. I was told after the event that Doctor Pinto had written a book regarding mental health, and that this book would not have made good reading for me at the time, due to his beliefs on mental health. However, I have never researched this, so cannot confirm if this is the case. At some point, I realised that my mouth had become extremely dry, and Mr Millet fetched a glass of water for me. It felt like I was on trial.

Dr Pinto kicked off the hearing by asking me a series of questions: "What symptoms do you still suffer, Mr Barden?" and "Were you given any medication?" This seemed like a stupid question at the time, as they had been provided with all the medical records prior to the hearing, but maybe they just wanted to trip me up. There were several other questions too, all aimed at trying to identify if I was going to incur permanent mental suffering from the attack.

Following this round of questions, which I feel I dealt with fairly well, they started to question me on my loss of earnings claim. There were periods prior to the attack where I was self-employed, and would invoice my customers for services. This meant that Wendy would submit my accounts when due. During their investigation, they had found an error in Wendy's latest submission, which was done after the attack. Apparently, I had earnt £1,380.87 that had not been declared to the tax office. This now meant that I was public enemy number one, even though in the info pack that had been submitted to them, it was suggested that this was disregarded due to the amount and the timing of when it was submitted. However the Right Honourable Eric Stockdale was clearly not having that, and I will quote some of the things that were said to me following his questions:

"We have all sorts of people in here claiming that after an attack they will never be the same again."

"This is tax payers' money, which is for the good of tax payers – that is those that pay their tax."

This was bad enough, but something that will stick with me forever was his final quote. He could clearly could see how upset I was, with my elbows resting on the table and my hands clasped together shaking, yet he said, "You should be grateful, a few years ago you would have got nothing."

Following this, I was asked if I had any questions, but I could not talk. I could not get any words out of my mouth. They were there, but I couldn't speak. Instead, I began to cry. I just sat there, crying and shaking, looking at the three people who I had put faith in to give me the acknowledgement that what I had been through was really bad, but instead I was feeling worse than at any point since the attack.

As I sat there, the Right Honourable Eric Stockdale looked up from his notes and over the top of his glasses, and said, "Is there anything else?" I just stood up and began to make my way from the room, followed closely by Wendy and Mr Millett. We made our way to the lift lobby, where Mr Millett clearly was not impressed with the conduct of the panel and my treatment. He let me know that there was one further action I could take, but this had never been tried before – I could go to a Parliamentary Ombudsman to complain.

I cannot even explain my thoughts as I left that building. Mostly it was anger, partly at my treatment, and partly down to this desire of mine to have someone say that they were sorry for what had happened.

In my desperation, I once again went to Victim Support and Ronni Ayers, who was a constant support to me and my family. After explaining about my experience, she wrote the following letter. The important part of this letter is in the second paragraph, where I was given one task – write a book. Well, Ronni, I have finally done it, so thank you for your encouragement.

Victim Support - West Essex

Kingsmoor House, Paringdon Road, Harlow, Essex. CM19 4QT.
Telephone: (01279) 641074 Fax: (01279) 422032
Registered Charity No. 802818-R-

Mr Darren Barden
101 Brocklesmead
Harlow
Essex
CM19 4PX

19th June 1998

Dear Darren

Here is a copy of the letter I have sent to Bill Rammell. It was not the easiest letter to write as there is so much to say and it is difficult to know what to include and what to leave out.

There is a task here for you - write a book! There is such a story to tell.

In talking to my V.S. colleagues, I have discovered that other people have made similar complaints about their treatment at Appeals. Can I have your permission to give them information which I believe our National Office will put with the other complaints to take up at some stage, presumably with CICA or the Home Office.

Bill Rammell does see constituents every 3rd Saturday, 10 - 12 noon at the Harlow Advice Centre, East Gate, also on the 1st Friday of each month, 5 - 7 pm at Adams House, opposite the Bus Station, so perhaps you (and perhaps, I) could see him to give him a fuller picture.

Let me know.

All the best to Wendy and the children.

Yours

Ronni,

CHAPTER 8

Life or Debt

When writing this book, I have placed a big emphasis upon the emotional impact that the attack had. However, there was another element to it – financial. Mentally, I was on my last legs, but financially this attack left me crippled.

Now, it is quite clear that I cannot blame the attack for everything that went on afterwards. As you will see, it was also responsible for some great stuff too, but a lot of what has happened over the past 21 years has been born out of my frustration of not having any recognition from the CICA, or there being anyone to blame for what happened.

Once I had failed in my attempt to secure any real financial compensation from the CICA, I needed to come up with other ways to get myself and my family back to normal. If you remember, I had always been a grafter, working at night for the extra money to give George that positive start in life, so the first thing I needed to do was take Dr Richard's advice and get myself back to work.

Getting a job has always come easy to me, as I know a lot of people, but it was time that I started to do something that I really wanted, rather than what I had to do. So, I began to look at opportunities in sales, where I felt I could flourish and give myself the potential to earn more than a basic wage.

I found a company that I liked the look of, called Allsigns, who sold safety signs to various different industries. I checked them out, borrowed my dad's car and drove to Doncaster in Yorkshire, which was about 3 hours from me. I pressed the buzzer and said, "Hello, can I have a job with you?" They were shocked at this approach, but after insisting on the directors meeting me there and then, and getting an interview on the spot, I came away with the job. Although they were based in Doncaster, my role was to cover the whole of the South of England. I worked there for almost 2 years, but in my desire to achieve I became ill and had to leave. I want to say that Allsigns

International were the most supportive company I could ever have wished for during my illness, and continued to be supportive even after I had eventually left.

After a short period of time, one of my old customers approached me about working for them. I took them up on this approach, but unfortunately the boss of the company was a bit of a bully to the staff there. On the one and only time he tried it with me, we parted company. So, following this, I started my own business with another one of my old customers. Once again things started out well, but then got difficult, which was brought about by my partner helping himself to the money we had earnt. So, when confronted with this difficult situation, I parted company and moved on to the next episode.

This may all sound a bit boring, but you will start to see a pattern emerging – where I get something good and it then goes wrong for one reason or another, which in turn was to bring about my eventual downfall. Looking back, it may have been wiser for me to take a simple job where I had a regular wage, but because I was chasing success to cancel out the negativity of the past couple of years, I just couldn't do it. I had to get that reward for my efforts. I had to show everyone that I could provide for my family and give them a good life, but every time I took 2 steps forward I would go 3 back.

My inability to deal with situations was starting to cost me dearly. Every time I parted company with my latest job or business, there were days and sometimes weeks where I was not earning money. This meant that, in order to survive, we would add food and other essentials onto our credit cards, and use up any overdraft facility we may have had. As I said at the start of this chapter, I cannot blame the attack for everything that went wrong for me, but my decisions were being made with this in mind – sometimes subconsciously rather than deliberately.

I ventured into several businesses with various people, but every time I was confronted with a difficult situation I would bail out, and every time without fail it would cost me financially. I eventually struck gold with a business that I had created, called Protective Safety. Protective Safety was created to provide clothing to the rail and construction industry, as well as PPE and other safety equipment. This began in my home, and after a fairly short time I was able to open a couple of small stores. Protective Safety was a small business, so when one of the biggest manufacturers in our industry approached me about supplying a leader in the traffic management field, I jumped at the opportunity. This particular company had wanted to purchase several traffic management products, but the manufacturers would only go via a recognised distributer – which in this case was me. Eventually I outgrew the stores, and moved the business into a much larger industrial unit, where it could grow even bigger.

Over a period of 5 years, I continued to build the business and recruited several members of staff, until I had about 6 or 7 people working with me. However, once again things became tough. I was not in control of the finances. I was growing the business, but avoiding difficult situations. My silent partners that I had used to finance the business in the first place had been all too silent, to the point that I forgot they were there, and just kept them out of any involvement with the business.

So, a situation was developing where I started to enjoy the fruits of my labour, and neglected the day-to-day running of my business. I had employed a friend of mine, and had given him the opportunity to be a general manager, which he did very well on my behalf. Unfortunately for me he was greedy, and started to take advantage of his position. With my focus being elsewhere, I didn't spot this until it was too late. He started to work very closely with our biggest customer, and eventually decided to leave. He joined the customer and formed a new business, copying my business model, and going into direct competition with me.

Ultimately, they failed. They had based their plans on my friend being able to run a business, and the strength of his relationship with all the customers. What they hadn't banked on was that the customers were loyal to me, and that my now ex-friend actually didn't have a clue about running a business. Their new set-up lasted just 10 weeks. Unfortunately, this meant they failed to pay the £36,000 that they owed me for previously supplied goods.

£36,000 was a huge amount of money, which we couldn't afford to lose. Following many attempts to retrieve the money, we failed, and as a result we had to shut the doors on the business. In the process, we damaged a lot of the very good relationships that had built up over the years.

This was when I started my meltdown. I had companies calling me, writing to me, and trying to visit me at my home. I had managed to secure a deal with another one of my old customers to create a new business, doing exactly the same as before, with a lot of the same suppliers and most of the old customers. However, whilst in the throes of setting up this new and exciting adventure I had a huge problem, which was that my old silent partners were suddenly not so silent.

They set about trying to retrieve their initial investment. As a result, I had people driving around the town looking for me, plus bailiffs knocking on my front door. The pressure was building, and eventually it became relentless. There was one occasion where two guys turned up at the premises of my new business, and spoke to a colleague of mine. They were looking for me. They had driven all the way down from Scotland just to sort it out. I received a phone call from my colleague to inform me of this, and promptly started to make plans to save myself from any future confrontation with these guys. Unfortunately, I then got a call from my neighbour, who informed me that two men fitting the same description were sitting in a car outside my house, after knocking at nearby houses, asking questions about me.

Now I was scared. I started to panic. I didn't know what to do or who to turn to, so I called Wendy to say do not go home to the house. We arranged for the kids to be picked up from school by my mother-in-law. I needed to keep them safe, as I didn't know what the outcome from these guys was going to be.

Whilst all of this was going on, I was in the midst of trying to set up the new business. Unfortunately, I was concentrating harder on dealing with the fallout from the old business than on the new one, meaning it was much harder to get the new business off the ground.

There was a funny moment in amongst all the dark days, where 2 guys knocked on the door showing me their warrant cards and sheriff badges – they were bailiffs, so naturally I was horrified that I'd answered the door to them. The reason this was funny is that they were stood on my doorstep, wearing the uniform that I had supplied to their boss some months previously. I urged them to call their boss and let him know whose door they had knocked on, which they did, and sure enough my good service levels paid off. They apologised for disturbing me, and left saying that no one from their company would call again.

Sadly, this huge financial burden would not go away. By this point, the continual flow of letters coming to our house was incredible, I would guess at possibly 15 to 20 letters every day, most of which were threatening some sort of action. Wendy and I would receive at least 10 phone calls per day, 7 days a week. They even tried to use our work numbers to get to us.

Now, this next bit may sound a bit strange depending on your view on things, but randomly in amongst all the threatening letters I received an envelope addressed to me. The envelope had been handwritten, all in capitals. I opened the letter and all that was inside was a newspaper cutting of an advert, with a yellow post-it note attached, saying, *"Why don't you speak to these, Dal?"* (this is what my family used as my abbreviated name).

The letter had been sent from my Auntie Janet, but I did not know why she had sent it, as we had not discussed our situation with anyone. At this point I was just trying to avoid things, hoping they would go away.

Little did I know that this piece of paper would later be our saviour, but for the time being I just placed it on the side and left it. The advert was for a debt management company called Spencer Hayes. Every day I would look at this newspaper cutting and move it backwards and forwards along the side, and sometimes move it to another part of the house, but for some reason it was always on show.

I truly believe that something inside me must have known that I needed this advert. I needed to make that call. But I just continued to allow the pressure to build. I continued to avoid dealing with the situation, because in my mind looking for help meant that I had failed once again. I had failed in my attempt to provide for my family. Making that call meant that I was once again weak, that I was not the man I thought I was, and that I had let everyone down.

During this journey, there have been some incredibly dark days – too many to write about in this short book, but I can assure you that there is nothing darker than the knowledge that you are hurting the people you love. Whilst writing this book I have laughed and I have smiled at certain things, but mostly I have cried, and in my opinion most of those tears are from guilt. I was the one causing Wendy and the kids all this pain and anguish. I was the one responsible for our downfall, and now more than ever, even with a way out, I was the one not making that bloody phone call.

If I was advising people now on what to do when times are hard, or things just get too much, I would be saying please, please, please speak to someone. Get help, don't let it build up. PLEASE DO NOT LET IT BUILD UP. When my family read this, and especially Wendy, it may come as a bit of a shock that it was during this period in my life where I first contemplated suicide, and this is the first time I have told anyone about this. I could see no way out from this situation, other than taking the problem away. In this case, the problem was me. Looking back, I know it would have been selfish of me to end it all. However, as you will read later, mental health issues leave you with no emotional control.

Finally, one day I walked into the living room, and Wendy was sitting there. She was sitting on the sofa, with pile of letters from all sorts of companies, telling us what they were going to do about getting their money back. I'd had enough. I picked up the newspaper cutting, removed the yellow post-it note, and made the call.

It was around 6.30pm when I did this, and it is possible that by doing it at this time, I was hoping no one would answer. However, they did, and I am now so glad for that. This was the beginning of our recovery from the depths of financial despair. The guy I spoke to was brilliant, and his advice would prove to be my awakening. The only issue was that, in order to get this company to act on our behalf, it was going to cost us £600 each.

What was logical at the time to this guy did not work in my head. He wanted me to stop paying any bills, any loans, anything at all, just so I could pay this £1,200 to his company. Eventually by not paying these bills we gathered the money to send him.

The effect was instantaneous. He immediately put the wheels in motion that we were going to enter what is called an IVA (Individual Voluntary Arrangement). An IVA is an agreement that is made with your creditors to pay off your debts over a period of time. It is a formal, legal debt solution. This means it is approved by the court, and your creditors have to stick to it. It's essentially a form of insolvency, but is different from bankruptcy. An IVA must be set up by a qualified person, called an insolvency practitioner. This will be a lawyer or accountant. The insolvency practitioner will charge a fee for the IVA, and these average at about £5,000, although at the time we only paid £1,200. The insolvency practitioner deals with your creditors throughout the life of the IVA, which is normally 5 years.

If you go to a debt management company for an IVA, find out how much they will charge you before you decide. A debt management company is likely to be more expensive, because they charge a fee on top of the insolvency practitioner's fees.

As soon as we entered into this arrangement, everything changed. The calls stopped. The letters stopped coming. Most importantly, the pressure went away.

We finally had our lives back, and were not being suffocated by the volume of pressure and anxiety.

Now, I am not going to tell you that all our troubles were over, far from it, but the feeling of having someone on our side dealing with this was immense. October being a pivotal month in our history, it seemed poignant for this to be the month where we entered into the IVA. This was a 5-year arrangement, where we had agreed to pay £750 per month in to our debtors via Spencer Hayes, to complete the debt.

After completing many forms and several income and expenditure forms, the £750 per month was what came out as the figure we could afford. It meant no more silly shopping sprees, no more wasting money on unnecessary things for the house or on the kids, it was all about the essentials. We now had to sit down once a week and plan the dinners for the week, so when we went shopping we just purchased enough for the week. We both had an allowance for things like haircuts, birthday cards and presents, which was a huge learning curve for us, but one we still adhere to even now, 7 years on (at the time of writing).

Although we entered into the IVA knowing it was for 5 years, the £750 every month soon became a burden and a weight upon our shoulders. The only way I could maintain these payments was to keep earning what I was earning at work, but once again problems were arising at work that needed me to deal with them. I started to revert back to type, and put my head in the sand and hoped they went away.

Ultimately, with self-preservation being a key factor, I decided to leave the business – which consequently had to close. This is not something that I am proud of, in fact it embarrasses me when I think of the opportunity I threw away. However, things had to change. Looking back, given the opportunity again I would have done things very differently, and I am sure I would have also been very successful. There were things in my world that needed to be dealt with though, which were taking over as my main focus.

After working very hard to keep up with the arrangement, even after my reduction in salary following the closure of the business, I decided that I needed to get control of the situation. This meant getting back my old self, but I couldn't do it alone.

I spoke to my parents, and asked if I could get a settlement figure from the debtors. My parents lent me £8,000, so I could finish the monthly payments, and be free of the IVA. In our post-stabbing life there were several memorable moments which changed our lives for the better. Along with the newspaper cutting, the loan from my parents was one of the most important. This really put us on the road to financial happiness. By no means were we well off, but the burden of paying our debtors every month had now gone, and we no longer had to answer to these faceless people making judgements on our every move. We could get a takeaway if we had some spare cash, and there was no having to disguise a spare £20 to treat ourselves. Although we were going to be in the IVA for the full 5 years, and this was going to be on our credit history for the full 6 years, we could start to plan for the future and start to live again.

CHAPTER 9

The Long Goodbye

There are a few key moments in my decline, and some were less noticeable than others, but they all contributed in their own way. On July 7th 2009 my brother-in-law passed away, after a long battle with an illness. This illness had eventually resulted in John having a double lung transplant, which was a first in the medical world, as this was the first time they had used both lungs from a crash victim.

This was an horrendous time for all of Wendy`s family, and I am sure you can understand that my emotions were pretty far from their thoughts, for obvious reasons. Now as this book is about my story, I will be a little bit self-indulgent. I had been taking Wendy to see her brother at a fantastic hospital called Papworth, in Cambridgeshire, about 40 minutes' drive from our house. I was also driving Babs and Herby to and from the hospital on many occasions. I was even going to the hospital on my own, so that John had someone there if others were not able to attend.

Now, please do not think for one moment that I am looking for any sort of gratitude. This was something I would do naturally. John was a great bloke, who I thought a lot of, and had many good times with, including holidays abroad. But in my mental state this was all going unnoticed. No one had considered that John was just a couple of years older than me, and it could have quite easily been me laying in that hospital bed.

Once again, I still had trouble with being selfish, even at the most inappropriate times No amount of other people`s grief or wellbeing was going to stop me putting my emotions first. It was during one of my visits to John, where he was sitting up and breathing on his own, that I had a chat about things. We had just moved house, and as of yet he had not seen the new house. My way of motivating him to get better was to point this out, and say come on get yourself out of here, you haven't seen our new house yet.

In my mind, I was saying the right things, but I am sure he was looking at me thinking what a wally! If I could get out of this hospital bed and come and see your new home then I bloody well would. John was fun and always brought a smile to everyone he met. You would always know when John walked in, because he lit the room up with laughter.

Watching John slowly get worse really hit me hard, but I needed to stay strong for Wendy. I so wanted to be there for her, as she had done for me on so many occasions before. In the main, no matter what thoughts were going on in my head, I was the ever-supportive husband, and I did everything I could to be there for her.

Still though, there was this little demon inside me. I kept thinking, why is no one thinking of me? Why does no one consider what I am going through? I was so selfish, but I could not control it. I started to overcompensate. I started to smother Wendy with affection, or what I thought was affection anyway. I made it so she couldn't move, just putting the kettle on was a job she should not have to do, so I would leap in to action, "I will do that". Taking her plate out to the kitchen was not a task my Wendy should have to do, "Stay there I will do that for you."

It is hard to say what was more important. Was it making sure that Wendy was ok in her hour of need, or me trying to be recognised for doing something good? I will never know, as somehow we just muddled through it and now just never talk about it. I do fear that one day Wendy will let me know exactly what she felt back then, but I hope it is in a letter in my grave, so I don't have to face up to the truth.

As the weeks went by, John's health worsened, and eventually there came a moment where his life support machine was to be switched off. I had been in Manchester in meetings that day, and was making my way across the M62 to Winsford in Cheshire where my hotel was, when the call from Babs came.

Babs told me that they were on the way to my house, and that the decision had been made to switch off John's life support machine. They were going to let Wendy know, and the following morning we were all going to the hospital to be there when the life support was switched off.

There was no way I was going to let Wendy go through this without me being there for her, and this was the moment the real Darren Barden kicked in. This was me with one thought on my mind, and that was the wellbeing of Wendy. No selfish thoughts, no what is in it for me, just get back and care for my wife. I told Babs I was on my way, and we agreed that they would wait until I got back from Manchester.

Unfortunately, it was at this moment that I realised my mobile battery was going flat.

I hurtled down the motorway, stopping at every service station until I found a shop that sold an in-car charger, so I could be available should the timing go wrong. Phone now being charged, I made my way down the M6 towards home, but sat in complete silence, no radio, just me and my thoughts.

I now know that these next few weeks were when my breakdown really began, but at the time there was no sign of this. I got home, stood strong and did what a real husband should do. I cared for the most important person in my world. As you can imagine, it was a tough time, but nowhere near as tough as the following day.

I had agreed to drive Wendy, Babs and Herby to the hospital, a journey that I would not wish on anyone. I was taking a mum, dad and sister to say goodbye. It is fair to say that no matter what conversation I started, it did not go far. There is no training for moments like this, and I am sure they were thinking "shut the fuck up" but nerves had kicked in, and talking is what I do.

I will avoid going into the details of those hours in the hospital, because that is not fair. Those moments belong to the individuals, and it is not my place to say what others were going through. However, I remember that the journey home was the worst car journey I have ever made. I had called and spoken to my dad in private to tell him the news, and I had a moment on the phone with him where we just stayed silent, mostly because I had no words.

I made one mistake when walking outside the ward with Herby, just after he started to talk about funeral arrangements. Being the 7th July, this was 1 week from my wedding anniversary. When Herby mentioned that he wanted a quick turnaround, I asked, "Not the 14th July, please Herby." Clearly the last thing on Herby's mind was my bloody anniversary. He dismissed my concerns, and understandably so, which was not taken in a bad way.

The days after John died were tough in our house. Wendy was off from work, and I seemed to be about the whole time making sure she was ok. But that bastard depression was sneaking up on me, and my mindset started to turn. Why was Wendy not saying, "Well done, Darren"? Why was there no recognition of my work? There are things that even today I truly hate myself for, and many of those things are from this period.

The day of the funeral had arrived, which we all attended as a family. Babs wanted me there all the way. At the time I thought that this was to make me feel a part of everything, but with grown up eyes now I realise she was dealing with Herby and Wendy's other brother Tony, as well as her own grief. Having me there for Wendy was one less thing she needed to deal with. I am glad I was involved, because it did help me support Wendy, but I am sure it was just agitating my darkest thoughts.

The funeral went about as well as a funeral could, and the service was lovely. We then moved to the wake, where friends and family could relax and have a few drinks. An old family friend of my in-laws had made it to the wake, and took centre stage because he was from their childhood. This really irritated me, especially when he called his own dad to get an old skateboard out of his garage and bring it to Wendy.

The significance of this skateboard was brilliant for Wendy and her family, but for me I was just thinking where the bloody hell were you at the hospital? Where were you at the funeral? You just bring some old family heirloom along and you're the greatest person ever. Eventually he got quite drunk, and proceeded to tell me how I should look after Wendy as she was one special person. I know what I was thinking, but just kept my mouth shut for a change.

After the wake, I had driven Babs and Herby to get a takeaway and then dropped them home, before making our own way back. This is when I let the vile, stupid Darren back in the room. I chose this moment to let Wendy know what I thought of the whole skateboard thing. What an idiot I was! To her credit, Wendy just slid her plate to the middle of the table and said, "I am not discussing this now".

You are probably thinking what an arse, and I agree and think even worse of myself, but I really had no control over these emotions. They just kept popping up and taking over. I know that this is when I should have got help, but I could only do that if I had recognised what was happening. I miss John a lot, and he will always be part of my happy memories. I sincerely hope he can look down and forgive me for my actions.

CHAPTER 10

Implosion

Looking back over the whole experience and my life since that day, I can now understand that the mental anguish from the attack had never really, gone away or been dealt with. That was until it finally all caught up with me, some 17 years later.

Almost within a few days of the attack, the depression had started to take control of my emotions. The anger as I went back to 101 for the first time, telling my loved ones that I wished I was dead, all this quite clearly was not me as a person. When my original counsellor had diagnosed me with clinical depression, I did not believe her. I could not accept that this one little moment in my life was going to take control of me, but all the experts said the same.

My counsellor referred me on to a psychiatrist, who was saying the same, but still I refused to believe them. I can remember saying to the psychiatrist, after she had reminded me that I was depressed, that "I was not depressed, I was bloody angry that someone had come in to my home and stabbed me over 20 times for no reason", but once again through all the sessions, and these very professional people trying to help, I just blocked them out.

As far as I was concerned, I had to have these sessions to help with my compensation claim, so I just needed to get on with it and tick that box. If only I had realised what they were trying to do, I may have not gone down the road I was later to travel.

As we speak now, mental health issues have really become a subject that we are happier to discuss, but go back a few years and people like myself did not really believe they existed. So, we were very dismissive of it. There was always a solvable answer to your problem, so surely there could not be anything that bad to make you feel so low?

At this point I would like to take some time to reflect on a few situations from the many that happened, which now I recognise as being part of the depression:

Immediately after the attack, I had the feeling I was invincible. On several occasions, I was driving and spotted a police car going the other way or just sitting there by the side of the road. I would undo my seatbelt, but in a way that was so dramatic it was almost pathetic. This may sound ridiculous to you, but I wanted them to see me. I wanted them to try and arrest me. I wanted that chance to say, "Do you know who I am? Do you know I had over 20 stab wounds?" I know looking back now it just sounds so stupid, but it was an emotion that I was not in control of.

Within a few weeks of the attack my mum and dad had decided that maybe we should get away from Harlow for a bit, so they arranged for Wendy, George and I to visit our friends in Holland. It was a really, nice trip but I couldn't help but feel like I was on the run from something. Nevertheless, upon our arrival back to England, my mum and dad had organised a beautiful little holiday in Spain.

Now, my mum and dad never had a lot of money, and it was at this time that my dad started to do extra work outside of his normal day job, to help support us. At the time, it did not register that he was doing this for us. I was just in my own little bubble and happy to receive his generosity.

So, Wendy, George and I, along with my sister Teresa, her husband Smithy, and my nephew Sam (who was a similar age to George) all flew off to Spain. The funny thing was that the resort was for retired people. It was a golden oldies hotel, picked by Mum and Dad to keep me as far away from any potential flash points as they could.

Although the weather was not so great, we generally had a good time, although there were a couple of moments when I lost the plot. This continual lack of control over my emotions at various times kept cropping up. For example, we were getting ready to go out for a meal, and I was using the bathroom in the apartment to get ready, whilst George was running around the legs of Wendy in the bedroom.

George now was pretty confident on his feet, as a one year old would be, so he came into the bathroom in a bit of a hurry – followed very closely by Wendy. As he arrived at my side he slipped on the wet floor and nearly fell towards the toilet. Instinct kicked in. My hand flew out, and I saved his head from hitting the rim of the toilet.

All of this was completely natural stuff, but as I pulled him up towards me to comfort him, there must have been something go off in my head. Wendy held out her arms, very slowly took George away from me, and closed the sliding door to the bathroom.

I am not sure what Wendy had seen, but there must have been a look in my eyes that she could recognise as trouble. I can remember most of what happened next, but still now I do not know what happened in my head. I grabbed the bathroom sink, shaking in anger. I could feel the rage overwhelming me, but I could not stop it. I started to punch everything in sight. I was kicking the walls, the door, even punching myself in the head.

I was crying, but it was anger. I do not know how long this went on for, but Teresa and Smithy had heard it in the adjoining apartment, and came to check on us. Wendy just passed it off as me having a little moment and sent them away. Eventually the moment passed, and I just sat there on the bathroom floor sobbing like a child, until Wendy and George appeared again at the now half open door. Somehow with the help of Wendy I composed myself, and finished off getting ready as though nothing had happened.

These moments of anger were to happen on several occasions whilst on this holiday, but as I became aware they were coming, I found myself being able to supress them as best I could.

Prior to flying out to Spain, my fantastic Auntie Kath had given us a few quid to put towards a meal whilst we were away, so we opted for a Chinese. I was having a bit of an issue understanding a part of the menu, so I called over the waitress to explain. She did this perfectly, but as she returned the menu to my hands, it suddenly went blank. I couldn't see the words on the menu, it was just a blur. It was happening again. The rage started to rise up through my body. I could feel it coming, and once again Wendy had also seen this. She calmly took the menu from my hands and guided my hands, so that they were both holding the edge of the table and very gently stroked my arm, whilst looking me in the eye, not saying anything but bringing me back to normal.

Looking back, there is so much of depression that is selfish, but clearly not in a deliberate way. Over the next few years I continued to have these moments, and as always Wendy was there to deal with the fallout or cover up the situation to the outside world. On several occasions she had told me how she was waiting for the day it all went wrong. Whatever I was holding back did eventually come out, but for 17 years I had kept it in. I just went about my life, doing my normal thing, trying to achieve some sort of success to prove that I was not a failure, until it finally caught up with me.

I was at a stage in life where things were apparently good. Wendy had worked her way up at Passmores Academy and was now in charge of finance, and earning a decent wage – to the point where she was the biggest earner in the house. If you had asked me as a man whether this bothered me, the answer was of course not! It all goes into the same pot, whoever earns it, but it was just another piece of the jigsaw that was being completed for my eventual meltdown.

George was doing well for himself too, earning a decent wage working in the railway, and he had a nice girlfriend, whilst Shannon was going along quite nicely at college with her friends and boyfriend. These were all pieces of normal life, but to me this all meant that I had become surplus to requirements. I felt as if my family no longer needed me. So, I started to create situations where they would have to prove their love for me. Unfortunately, they didn't even notice.

At first, I would ask either George or Shannon to help me with something that I could really do on my own, just to see if they would help. Now, being young and still at the stage of throwing their arms around whenever they were asked to do anything there was only ever going to be one outcome. But in my mind, they made it difficult because they did not care and sometimes I would think that they were pushing me so I would go away forever. This was only going on in my head, but it was real to me, and as a consequence made the situation worse.

My plans started to become more important to me. I started to look at why they no longer wanted me around, and this manifested into me blaming Wendy for everything. The one person who was there through everything, who supported me, comforted me and kept me going, was now at fault.

I convinced myself that Wendy`s love was elsewhere, and I do not mean she was having an affair, but as far as I was concerned she no longer loved me or even liked me. I felt like she had replaced me with her work and her workmates. To me she clearly thought more of these people than me, and to be honest the way I was behaving you could see why.

I was vile. I was really hurting Wendy emotionally. I believe that hurt will always remain, but she hides it, as it is easier to believe it was not me that was doing these stupid things.

As an example of how poor my behaviour was, I would call Wendy at work to try and catch her out. What I was trying to catch her out at, I do not know. I would call her at 4.35pm, knowing she finished work at 4.30pm, asking whether she had left yet. Wendy was in a senior role, and could not always leave on time, but now this became an issue for me. I would be there waiting, just looking at the clock, working out how long it would take her to walk to her car. Then, allowing for a little bit of traffic, even trying to work out exactly how many cars were actually on the road at that time of day. I would become anxious if she did not meet my timescales. My anxiety then led to anger, where I would begin to do things like tip hot water away and put cold water in the kettle, so she would have to wait for her tea when she got home from work. My emotions were out of my control. In my head, Wendy no longer cared about me. Even worse, I thought she detested me.

Looking back, I suppose I should be grateful that there was never any physical anger towards Wendy. No, instead I was saving that for someone else. We were out for a friend's birthday party at a place called Billy Jeans, in Epping. It was a nice little club that played all the music we had grown up with from the 80s, and in the main was full of similar aged people, all having a good time.

It had just got to midnight when I noticed 3 guys walk in. They went and stood at the bar, but with their backs to it. They were just looking out at everyone having a good time. Now, I am not an expert, but these 3 guys were not drunk. To me it seemed that they were in this club for one reason only – and that was to cause someone some trouble. As I was watching them scanning the place, I saw the guy on the left mouth the words, "watch this" to his mate next to him.

He then began to walk around the edge of the club, around all the happy people enjoying themselves, and as he passed the back of Wendy he thrust his groin into her bum, knocking her into the table.

This was my cue. The red mist came down. 17 years of not being able to vent my anger was about to release. In my head, this was the moment when it started, when everything I had held back came out.

I marched over and pushed the man away from Wendy. He immediately tried to bump her again, so I grabbed his throat. He had this blank look on his face, it was like I wasn't there. At this point

Wendy had thought that some guy had bumped into her as he was passing, and I was overreacting to it, so she was absolutely livid with me. However, I wasn't the least bit interested in what Wendy was thinking. I was solely focused on this idiot, and in my mind I was going to kill him. I can tell you that if I could have got the bottle from the table to stab his neck, I would have carried on until he was dead! I so wanted this guy dead. In my head I just kept stabbing the bloke's neck with the now broken bottle.

Between Wendy and the bouncer, I was taken out of the club. After a couple of attempts to get back in, I eventually gave in to Wendy's shouts, and went back to our car for a less than happy journey home.

Wendy knew this day had been coming. she knew someone was going to pay the price for my attack, but I suppose she had never envisaged it happening in front of her work pals on a pleasant night out. I had gone too far this time. I had embarrassed her. We arrived home and sat at the dining table, with Wendy crying and having a go at me, but I just sat there thinking how I could get back to that club and finish the job.

Unfortunately for George he came home with his girlfriend, and walked into the dining room (full of happiness after a good night out) to see us sitting there. Quite clearly something was very wrong. I wanted George to get me back to Epping so I could deal with this bloke. George, not knowing what to say or do, agreed. As you can imagine, Wendy put him straight!

The next few weeks were spent with me mostly in my own world, just contemplating the future. There were many times when I would storm off after a discussion with Wendy. I now knew I was no longer loved. I was no longer needed by anyone. I could no longer prove to anyone that I was not a failure, because no one cared. It was at this point that I started to work out how things would go if I was not around anymore.

In my head, I had gone through how my family would cope with me not being there. I had even worked out how much time off work Wendy would have, and how she would respond to people as they asked her how she was. I started to map out George and Shannon's next few years, as they came to terms with not having their dad around.

I needed to know all this, because I could then go in the knowledge that they would all be ok in the end. I was trying to work out how long they would grieve for and how this would manifest itself. I started to look closer at the people around us, to see who I could trust when I am not here, who would put my family first rather than their own interests.

I developed a hatred for a couple of guys who I thought would use the situation to try and win Wendy's affection. This became a real problem for me, to the point where I thought they were already trying to position themselves in case I was not around. I then escalated this to the point where I thought Wendy was encouraging them, just in case I was not around. I started to try and catch Wendy out, even more so than before. She was obviously keeping secrets from me, clearly leading some sort of double life in preparation for my demise.

I even took the trouble to place a single red rose on Wendy's car whilst she was at work. I left no name, just a message saying something stupid which could have been read in 2 ways. In my head, I knew she was going to keep this a secret from me, because she would think that this was from the real love of her life.

When I say that there are things that I did that were vile, this was one of them. To me I was catching Wendy out, but to Wendy this was her worst nightmare. Wendy knew that if this rose was from a secret admirer, in my state of mind it would tip me over the edge. She questioned all the girls she worked with about what to do.

Wendy really did not want to come home and tell me that someone had left a rose on her car. If you were to ask Wendy now what were the worst moments during my breakdown, then this would be right up there. It may sound like we were both being a bit silly, but I was slowly going off my head, and Wendy was continually trying to avoid any situation that would set me off. Eventually I confessed and tried to play this off as a show of my love, but Wendy knew. She knew that this was just another episode in my decline.

So, I carried on. Everyone was becoming a threat, everyone knew I was going, but didn't want to say anything. I couldn't trust anyone or believe anything they said, but above all they knew I was a failure, and that I had let everyone down.

This low self-esteem was tiring, because it was relentless. It was every single day. Most hours of the day were just a struggle. At night, I would go to bed and somehow talk to Wendy, but in a way that was having a go at her, then made out it was her fault. Then I would aggressively throw the sheets back, stomp out of the room, slamming doors and go downstairs in a rage, leaving Wendy quite often just crying herself to sleep.

If it were possible to go back in time and erase certain things from this period in my life, I would take away from the memory of Wendy. I know none of this was the real me. I know I was not in control of my emotions, and there was nothing I could do to stop it, but it must have scarred Wendy for life. Writing about my whole story has been a great help, but I still get angry with myself over the pain I must have caused during this spell.

I had started to accept that there must be a problem, rather than everyone hating me, and eventually plucked up the courage to book an appointment with my doctor. In typical fashion, it was 3 weeks away from the phone call, but at least I had booked it.

This became the start of the recovery, but there was still a way to go before I could believe in myself again. I am not sure if just booking the appointment had helped, but I started to have the odd day where

I felt better. I could smile without feeling guilty, I could enjoy people's company again, but as the days ticked past and the appointment became closer, I started to go backwards again.

On the morning of what was now the biggest and most important day of my life, Wendy was getting ready for work, but was worrying about her boss Vic. Wendy had worked with Vic for nearly 10 years at this stage, so knew him well, so when his brother tragically died she felt his pain.

The day of my appointment was the same day as Vic's brother's funeral. Wendy wanted to send him a message, to show how we were all thinking of him and his family on such an awful day. Wendy asked me for some words, as I was normally quite good with that sort of thing. Unfortunately, I was of no help whatsoever. I was in my own world, suffering my own grief, so who the bloody hell cared about Vic and his poxy family? Because of my reaction to Wendy wanting to write this text message, I believe Wendy opted not to send a text. This is really sad, because it really would have been the right thing to do.

I have since spoken to Vic about this moment, because I always felt bad, even though he would have never been aware of the moment. I had to say sorry because it played on my mind and was one of the demons I had to get rid of.

It really upset me at the time that Wendy could even consider a text to Vic when I was on my way to being certified as insane. Vic is one great guy and had his moment on the TV documentary *Educating Essex* as the head teacher, and therefore had been recognised for all his good work, whilst no one gave a damn about little old Darren Barden. I was attacking the heart of Wendy, and I will probably never forgive myself for this for as long as I live.

CHAPTER 11

Fernandez

Now I am not sure about you, but when I book a doctor's appointment, I like to see my own doctor. At that time, my doctor was named Dr. Fernandez. In my state of mind I felt I needed to speak to someone who knew me, someone who at least somewhat understood me and what I'd been through.

I arrived at the surgery earlier than my 10am appointment, and made my way to the screen where you can wash your hands with the sanitiser, and book in using the automated system. As I registered myself, the screen said that I was seeing a different doctor, so I went to reception to ask what was happening. The lady just pointed out that my new doctor was a trainee, but that Dr Fernandez was going to be in the meeting.

Now, to most normal people this would not be a problem, but at this stage I was far from normal, and I started to wind myself up over the fact that there was going to be someone else in the room. As the buzzer went and my name came up on the LED screen telling me what room to go to, I quickly got up and made my way to room 3.

Upon entering the room, I saw the stranger sitting behind my doctor's desk, and my doctor was sat on a spare chair in the corner of the room. They both greeted me nicely, and Doctor Fernandez explained that the guy behind the desk was training, whilst Dr Fernandez was overseeing him. Clearly, they were not prepared for the volley of foul and abusive language that came out of my mouth in response. With an incredibly aggressive and rude tone, I began my rant, "I have waited 3 weeks to see my doctor to tell him how I am fucking nuts, and I walk in here to see a fucking stranger. Now can I suggest you get up and swap seats, so I can tell my doctor how I am on the verge of fucking killing myself, rather than some fucking stranger who I have never met before!" I finished with, "Do it now or I am fucking off out of this room, and you will never see me again because I will be dead."

I am so ashamed of myself for this, but at the time I was livid. It was another example of not having someone acknowledge the seriousness of what I was going through. Looking back, I am surprised they didn't just call the police, but to my surprise they got up and swapped seats.

Doctor Fernandez got me to take a seat, as I was still pacing around his room at this point, "So, Darren, what seems to be the problem?" At this point I just started to sob uncontrollably. I couldn't breathe, I couldn't speak, and then it happened again. The rage came up through my body again, I began rocking in the chair, and I started to punch myself in the head. I started to shout obscenities at myself repeatedly, still rocking back and forth. I can imagine that the poor trainee was pretty horrified by this!

I am not sure how long this went on for, but it felt like hours. Eventually I spoke. "I'm so low," I said. "You won't believe how low I am, so low, so alone." The doctor was brilliant, his voice just calming me down so he could understand what I was saying.

"Ok, Darren. What is causing you to feel this low?"

"I don't know. I'm just so lonely, I want to end it all."

It was clear to him that I needed more than the allocated 4 or 5 minutes you get at these appointments, so he gave me the phone number of an organisation called MIND, and told me to ring them as soon as I could. He also asked me to return to the surgery in 2 days' time, so that I could talk to him for as long as I needed, before writing down an appointment date on a piece of paper and handing it to me. I took the note and agreed to call MIND as soon as I got home.

I cannot explain how huge a moment opening up to the doctor was for me, even with the shameful entrance, but I now discovered that I had another challenge to overcome. My first thought was to call Wendy as soon as I got to my car. Wendy was at work, but I needed to tell her I had done it, I had seen the doctor. In my mind, this would help her too, as it would be the first step to feeling better.

As Wendy answered the phone all joyful and happy, I just sobbed. I cried and cried, and once again was having trouble speaking. Eventually we spoke, and I told Wendy about my appointment and how I had behaved, and in typical fashion Wendy just smoothed it over, saying that she was sure the doctors were used to it and had seen worse.

Upon my return home, I tried to call MIND using the number he gave me, but I was met with an answer phone message directing me to their website. I was a bit frustrated, as I was expecting to speak with someone, not fill in a form on a website, but it appeared at the time that this was my only option.

The completing of this form was possibly one of the lowest points during my whole breakdown. The questions that I was asked and the answers I gave were as honest as I had been with myself for a long time, and the reality of the situation hit me right in the face.

I cannot remember the actual words, but there were questions on self-harm, and then there were questions around suicide. I felt as if I had hit rock bottom there and then. I was sitting in front of a computer screen, being asked whether I had thought about taking my own life. When I answered yes, I was given the following question:

How often do you think about this?

- Every now and then?
- Once a month?
- Once a week?
- Once a day?
- More than once a day?

I ticked the last answer. There were so many questions, and so many things that were asked of me, that I really realised I had a massive problem. As hard as it was, and I am telling you pressing the "SUBMIT" button was one of the hardest things I have ever done on a computer, it was also a huge relief. I felt like I had finally contacted someone for help. Following this, a message popped up on the screen, saying that there were concerns for my welfare and that someone would be in touch within 24 hours. That was years ago, and to this day I have never had a call from MIND or anyone connected with them...

This all occurred on the Monday, right at the start of the week, so I sat back and waited for the call. I had just told the computer I was contemplating suicide every day, so someone would surely pick up the phone to save me. Tuesday came and went, and then on Wednesday I had my return visit to Dr. Fernandez. I must admit that sharing my thoughts with the computer had helped in some way, maybe it was just owning up to my issues, I don't know. So, when I walked back in to Dr Fernandez room again I was feeling a bit better about myself. Remember he had booked this appointment for me himself, saying I would have his undivided attention, and that I could have as long as was needed. Finally, I had progress! Well that was until I opened his door. Sitting in the corner of the room was a lad of about 20, who Fernandez introduced as a trainee.

I quite calmly asked the trainee to leave and go and get a cup of tea, or do whatever he needed to do, whilst I spoke with my doctor on his own for a while. Once again I felt betrayed, as if no one was taking me seriously. I feel now that maybe I was just one of thousands of people going through something traumatic, and we all had our own agenda, so we seemed to just hop on the 'Mentalist Production Line' until you either fell off or were lucky enough to be saved.

The one good thing I took from this appointment was the explanation of what I was suffering from. Depression is a chemical imbalance in the brain, where if my brain was an old-fashioned set of scales, then one side was hitting the table and the other was up in the air.

Doctor Fernandez had a solution for me, in the form of tablets – 50mg Sertraline. He explained that the tablets were not what I called happy pills or antidepressants. Instead they were to bring the chemicals within my brain back in line with where they should be.

He gave me a prescription for 2 months, as I needed to take them daily for some time in order for it all to start working. Dr Fernandez also booked my next appointment for when the tablets were due to run out. He said that if I needed to then I could call him, and he would call me back as soon as he was free. This was an offer that I took up on a few occasions, and true to his word he always called me back.

CHAPTER 12

Magic Pills

In theory, the answer to all my problems was in this little cardboard box. All I had to do was open the box up and start taking the tablets once a day. Unfortunately, this was not to be something I could do, as it felt like admitting failure. If I took the tablets, then my attackers would have won. They would have beaten me, and I could not let that happen. I placed the tablets on the kitchen window sill, on their edge, so I could see them every time I entered the room.

Every day I would look at this box, and every day I would say no don't do it, don't give in. I had convinced myself that if I started to take the pills then I would never come off them, and that they would have control of my mind and my mental state. So, as you can imagine, my moods and my general wellbeing stayed exactly the same. I continued to upset Wendy on a daily basis. I continued to have bouts of anger, and days where my existence was irrelevant.

Then, on Boxing Day I was having Christmas dinner at Wendy's parents' house. Herby had been suffering with a heavy cold for many weeks. There was a moment when myself and Herby were at the dining table, just the 2 of us – as the girls were in another room, and through his croaky, sad voice, he said, "They did not prepare me for this in old age." Clearly the cold had got to him, and it was really sad to see. There was real sorrow in his voice, as if he was telling me something.

Herby knew I loved his daughter more than anything in the world, and if anything was to happen to him he knew I would be there for her, but at that moment I couldn't even take care of myself. If anything was to happen to Herby, I would be useless. His message, even if unknowingly, was for me to get myself sorted and look after his daughter how he knew I could. That was it, the decision was made. I had finally realised that I wasn't doing this for me, I was doing it for the most important person in my world.

The following day I sat in my living room, opened the box, and with a sip of water took the first tablet. I cried, but I am not sure if they were tears of sadness because it had beaten me or tears of happiness, because I had taken the first step to "Skipping to the Good Bits". As always, who was there with her arm around me, making sure I was ok? Wendy. We just sat there in silence for a few moments, I'm not sure why, but it was just the right thing to do.

I am not sure if I was expecting a magic wand to be waved, but that was not the case. In timely fashion, my best friends Stuart and Rachel arrived that day to spend some time with us. They had travelled down from Hornsea in East Yorkshire, after speaking with Wendy and hearing about my wellbeing.

As I took the first tablet, I had a little thought that maybe it would work before they arrived, but 2 hours was clearly not long enough. I needed weeks, not hours. Stu and Rach arrived, and after the small talk about what was going on in each other's lives, we decided to go for a walk.

Stu and Rach had grown up in the area that I was now living in, so this gave us the opportunity to take a trip down memory lane. Stu and Rach understood us as a couple, they knew what me and Wendy were like, and they too had been through a story worthy of its own book.

These three had come with an objective, they had an agenda, and as they had planned at some point it would be just be Stuart and I walking and talking. This gave Stuart the opportunity to get to the root of my problem, and to make sure I was ok. I am not going to speak of the reasons Stu and Rach understand my situation, because I am hoping they are inspired by my own book to share their story, in a book that I would certainly read.

As we walked and talked, things became a lot clearer and I started to feel more relaxed. As always, my walks were to involve a pub. We stopped at the first pub on our route, The White Horse, which gave us the opportunity to speak together rather than in two groups of two. To my shock, both Stuart and Rachel had a drink with me, and by this I mean an alcoholic drink. Neither Stuart nor Rachel had drunk any form of alcohol for over 2 years now.

This was another amazing example of how people did actually care about me. But in my mental state, I was unable to see it at that time. This was an incredible day. We visited a couple of pubs, and had several drinks, before heading back to the house for dinner and more drinks. It was the most relaxed I had been for years.

So, I'd done it. I had taken the first tablet. I knew why I was doing it, and I had my closest friends with me to share the moment. Taking the second tablet the following day was almost a celebration. I was actually looking forward to it. What I had not realised was that quite a few of my friends had been on these tablets at some stage in their lives, but were always too embarrassed to say anything to anyone.

Over time, I started to feel different. I was telling everyone about how I was a mentalist, but was being saved by these magic pills. Off the back of my openness, people were telling me all their woes, and why they were on medication too, or how they eventually came off the pills – which was something I was yet to experience. For now though, I was just happy to be feeling better about myself, and enjoying waking up in the morning next to the most incredible woman in the world.

Over the next few weeks I told more and more people about my situation, and in return they started to share their own issues with me. This was something that I really enjoyed. I felt that we had things in common. I was feeling like I could help, not with advice, but just by lending them my ear. Not only was I giving others the opportunity to share, but I was releasing a lot of my issues as well.

CHAPTER 13

The Good Bits

Whilst taking those tablets set me off on the road to recovery, after what was to be described as a mental breakdown, there are many reasons I am here writing my story for you to read. Obviously the most important reason is my wife Wendy. Her support, patience and love has been greater than anything I could have wished for.

I have already given my acknowledgements at the front of the book, so I don't want to repeat what has already been said, but I do want to tell you how coming out of the other end of this story has given me the strength to write this book.

As the tablets started to work, I found myself feeling good about life. Getting up in the mornings was no longer a chore. I was really becoming me again. Now, I am not going to kid you that all was resolved at this point. Far from it, I had the odd day where certain things would get to me. A good example of this was after a fantastic night out in London with Wendy and Shannon, seeing a friend's daughter in a band. For some reason I had forgotten to take my tablet, and only announced this in the car on the way to the gig.

As it was, we just joked about it on the way there. We had a great night laughing and seeing several bands made up of university graduates, who were all very talented. On our way back to the car, whilst Shannon and I were messing about pushing each other from side to side, Wendy suggested that we grab a McDonalds.

It was getting close to midnight as we placed our order at the counter. We waited for some time for our order to come out, which I enquired about a couple of times, as others were getting food and leaving fairly quickly compared to us. The young lady behind the till explained that they were just waiting on the chicken, but acknowledged how long we'd been waiting.

After about 10 minutes, which is quite a long time in a fast food outlet, I once again enquired as to when I would get my food. At this point the very nice lady put a couple of bits in a paper bag, and placed it to one side, explaining that this was my food and the chicken was on its way. I thanked her and just waited at the counter, by this time Wendy and Shannon had taken a seat just behind me. As I stood there waiting, another member of staff walked along and looked in the bag that the girl had prepared for us, and then took out one of the items.

Now, after waiting for well over 15 minutes, I was less than happy. The old devil, rage, started to rear its ugly head again. I raised my voice at the girl that had prepared the bag. Pointing angrily at the guy who had helped himself to my stuff, I said, "Excuse me but that guy has just taken my food!" To be fair the nice young lady was completely oblivious to this, and just shrugged her shoulders, which then forced me to raise my voice more.

Now, I still feel I was correct in questioning what was going on, but my tone and my attitude had changed dramatically. A voice from the queue behind shouted, "Your aggression is making me feel sick!" She was right, but the red mist had descended, so I shouted back across all the other people in there, "What the fuck has this got to do with you?" This then prompted the guy behind me to say, "Ok, mate, calm down, there is no need for that". Now in full dickhead mode, I responded with, "And you can shut the fuck up as well!"

As my food turned up and I took my seat with the now highly embarrassed Wendy and Shannon, I suddenly lost my appetite and just sat there like a naughty little kid with my arms folded. I think that if we had not been in such a public place then both Wendy and Shannon would have cried. However, I am pleased to say that was the last time I had any form of relapse, and that was many years ago now.

Following that, with my lesson learnt, there was never going to be a day where I missed my tablets again. However, after being on these tablets for nearly a year, I felt that it was time to come off them.

Rather than taking the advice of many, I just stopped taking them. Now according to every expert, and Wendy, this was not a good move – so back on them I went, but promptly booked myself in to see Doctor Fernandez again. His advice was to miss every other day, and then every other 2 days until they were gone, and just monitor my moods.

I am so pleased to say that from the very last tablet until present day, there has never been any need for me to go back to the tablets. In fact, my life has completely changed, and for the better in many ways.

As I was feeling so good about life, it gave me time to look at what I really wanted, and especially from my work. I made the decision to change my employment. I needed to change, but what could I do? I had started to register with various employment agencies, in the hope that one would be creative with my experience and get me something different but challenging.

I received a phone call from an employment agency, asking me if I would look at a job with a company called Hilti. Now I had heard of Hilti, as one of my friends had worked for their competition some years previously, so after consulting with him I decided to go for it.

The interview process was long. I had a telephone interview, followed by an assessment day in central London. This is where you have several interviews, followed by the opportunity to show off your selling skills, in a style like The Apprentice. Luckily this was me in my element, showing off in front of people, and just generally enjoying the whole day.

This was then followed by a day out with one of the experienced account managers, for them to assess me and for me to see if this was what I wanted to do. I would like to say thank you to Gregor – who monitored me, as it opened my eyes as to what I wanted to do for a living.

That was the day I not only fell in love with the job, but it was also the day I found the real Darren Barden again. I can remember having 2 more interviews after that, and rather than just sitting back hoping I had got the job, I began to fret a bit. I really wanted this job, and I really wanted this way of life. I can assure you that everyone around me would now say they are so glad it worked in my favour.

After getting the good news that I was successful, and I could start my new role in December 2015, I entered into a period of training for the new position. This meant going back into a classroom after 30 odd years.

I would be lying if I said I was not nervous, but I can tell you that my nerves were misplaced. Going back to learning was brilliant, I could not get enough of it! I was meeting loads of great people of all ages from all over the world, and began to make some great friendships, which are still in place today.

I suddenly found out that there really was an employer who not only believed in having a good work/life balance, but actively encouraged it. This might sound like I am just trying to keep my current employer sweet, but Hilti are truly a brilliant organisation to work for. They have helped me to find myself again, and that has put me in a position to write my story.

As you have read, I have cried more than I have ever cried whilst writing this book, but that has also helped me get "closure" on many things in my life. It has also opened my eyes to many things that I have gone through, and things that I have put others through. In turn, this has made me more aware of my own actions.

Over the past couple of years, I have enjoyed every minute of my life, and I am sure the impact of that has been noted at home with Wendy, George and Shannon. We have laughed so much, and enjoyed doing so many things together, and I am pleased to say that George now works at Hilti and is doing very well. Shannon now works at Passmores Academy, in a different department to Wendy, but it does mean that they get to enjoy mother and daughter time as well.

Going forward, I would like to use my knowledge to help others. I want to get around to various organisations, and share my experiences, in the hope that I can inspire others who are suffering as I was.

In particular, I would like to bring awareness of mental health issues to the construction and rail industries. I would like to bring about change in people's behaviour towards mental health, and hope to take away the stigma that is attached to mental illness.

As I have said, I am no doctor, and I am certainly not a counsellor, but I would love to help others get through difficult times. Some people do not have the benefit of beating depression, and fixing their financial situation, but I have survived all of that. As Ronni Ayers used to tell me, "Darren, you are not a victim. You are a survivor!" In line with this, I will be making myself available as a guest speaker to share my experiences and help others. So, if you are connected to an organisation and feel I could be of help, please get in touch. You can do this via my Facebook page or my website (www.darrenbarden. com). When carrying out these events I keep them fun and interactive with my audience, so the whole thing is enjoyable for all.

I have also begun work on putting together some classes, which I can take to young people in schools around the UK. I would like to educate school leavers about how a career in sales can be as fruitful as any other industry. The one thing you will find with any salesperson, is that they'll all tell you this wasn't their first choice of career. It is nearly always the case that they fell into the role by mistake, or through other circumstances. If I can help give the next generation the confidence to go out and follow their dreams, that would be a great legacy to leave behind.

If you are connected to a school, college or university and feel one of these courses can be of assistance, then please get in touch using the details mentioned, or on the back of this book. The subject will be fun and very interactive. Who knows, it may even help inspire the next generation of entrepreneurs!

I would also ask that if you are a business owner or are involved in a business that takes advantage of having a sales force, then there is scope for us to work together and get young people involved in sales.

My future is now the brightest it has ever been, and for that I am extremely grateful. I enjoy getting up every day, seeing new people, and working with some of the nicest people around. With all the changes over the past 21 years, Wendy has told me that I will definitely retire at Hilti. If Wendy says that, then that is exactly what is going to happen!

Thank you so much for taking the time to read my story, and I hope that it can inspire you in some way. However far you have fallen, please remember that there is always hope, and there is always a way back.

Appendix

WENDY'S STORY

On the evening of 7th October, like most nights, George was up teething. Due to his ability to live off just a few hours of sleep, our spare room was converted to a space. This meant that Darren was not disturbed every evening. At around midnight, I was pacing up and down the bedroom rocking and bobbing George with the continual, "shhhhh, shhhhh, shhhhh" just trying to get him to sleep. Then, I heard a knock at the front door, and seconds later heard Darren stumble down the stairs.

Once the door was opened I could hear that something was going on at the base of the stairwell. I thought I could hear screams, but couldn't work out what it was. I kept myself in the bedroom, now really scared of what was going on. It sounded like some nutter had knocked on our door, and was screaming at Darren for help. Listening, trying to work it out, it wasn't long before I realised that all was not well. I heard someone screaming for the police, and then it dawned on me that it was Darren and he was on the phone.

I ventured downstairs gingerly, with George in my arms. I normally wear glasses, but at night I leave them by the side of the bed. Luckily for me, this meant that when I got to the front room, the extent of what had happened was a bit blurry, so when I eventually got close to Darren it seemed to me like he'd been beaten up. I quickly ran back upstairs to grab my glasses, to return to his aid.

By the time I returned, Darren had finished on the phone, and was sitting in the corner of the front room feeling cold. I quickly put our heating on full blast. I could see that Darren had blood running down his face, so I grabbed the nearest thing to me, which happened to be a tea towel, hoping it would help. Unfortunately, it did not. I had placed George on the sofa, and because Darren was shielding his face from the blood, George thought he was playing 'peek a boo'. For a few moments this did put a smile on Darren's face.

At this point I thought I'd grab Darren a quilt to keep himself warm, but halfway down the stairs I looked at our quilt, and I decided that I need to change it for the spare one, as I didn't want to get blood on my favourite cover. It's amazing what shock can do to you. As I continued back down the stairs, reality hit me. I hadn't taken much notice before, as getting to Darren was my priority, but this time I walked slower down the stairs and faced what was now a crime scene, one you could only normally imagine, but this was real.

I froze on the stairwell. My heart sank, what the fuck?! There was blood all up the wall and on the floor, where I later learnt that the attack had occurred. I was only there a few seconds, but it felt like ages, I then looked down at the quilt and carried it to the living room. Just as I covered Darren, there was another knock at my door. Unknowingly to me it was a couple of our neighbours who had heard the commotion and were checking up on us.

I thought they were coming back for a second go, so I just screamed at them that the police were on their way and to leave us alone. The neighbours must have realised that I would not be opening the door, and quickly retreated. It seemed like as soon as they left there was yet another knock on the door. Again I shouted, but it was the police this time. I asked them to post their ID through the door, as I wasn't believing anyone.

From that point onwards, the room seemed to be filled with lots of people coming in and out, but they were all moving in slow motion, while I sat on the sofa with George. Darren's parents arrived, but were not allowed in the front room, so I went upstairs with them. I sat on the bed watching their mouths move, but not taking in anything they were saying. They got some bits ready for George so that I could go with Darren to the hospital, and at this point I got myself dressed.

Once the ambulance crew were happy to transport Darren to the hospital, I left George with Sue and Pete, and made my way to the ambulance with Darren. Considering the time, I remember that it was quite bright outside, the sky was so clear. As we sat inside the vehicle I remember Darren was still trying to make light of the situation, he kept asking the police and ambulance crew to put the sirens on. It was his first time in an ambulance, and he wanted to have the full works – lights and sirens. The crew I think were getting bored of him asking, so I remember the driver shouting back at one point, "Tell him we have just gone through a red light, that should keep him happy!"

We entered the hospital through the A&E entrance and were taken to a room where 2 nurses cleaned Darren up and began the task of stitching his wounds. It wasn't until now that it dawned on me exactly what had happened to Darren, and in our home. I was informed that if the wound on his back had just been a few millimetres deeper, I would be writing this as a widow, and George would be without his father.

I felt sick and weak at this point, but I put on a brave face, as Darren needed me to be by his side. I wasn't there for long, as the police needed to speak to me. I was escorted out of the room and they sat me in the corridor. The police officer, in a nice soft voice, started to ask me questions about what had happened. All I was interested in was asking if they had turned my heating off, and if they had locked the house up properly; as I walked out of the house with nothing – no keys or my bag.

The officer kept reassuring me that he would radio through with my request. Once I was happy with the answer, he then continued with his questioning: Had I had an affair? Had I borrowed money from a loan shark? Was I in any other money troubles? I couldn't believe that they thought I could be the cause of this horrific attack! I was shocked that they could ask me such questions, but after the event I understood that they had to rule out any possibilities.

I answered all the questions with quite an abrupt NO, asking if I could return to my husband, as I needed to make sure he was ok, but also because I didn't feel safe. I wanted to be by his side.

On my return to the room, Darren's back had been stitched. They had to do a double layer of stitches as the wound was so deep. He was now leaning over what could only be described as a metal trough, and they were rinsing the blood out of his hair. As I got close, all I could see was a stream of blood flowing past.

Watching the nurses stitch his head was possibly the worst thing ever. They would inject first to numb him, but as he looked at me you could see the severe pain this caused. After quite a few injections, he decided that the pain was just too much, and made the decision to let them stitch without numbing.

I remember looking at his head, there were just so many small wounds, and as I pointed out some they missed, Darren would tell me (in a joking way) to keep quiet, but I kept on finding them! Eventually they finished and we were transferred to a cubicle, at which point both my mum and Darren's dad were there, waiting to make sure we were ok. I just sat there staring into space. What had happened? Why?

My mum had received the dreaded call from Pete (Darren's dad) and made her way straight to the hospital. Unfortunately, my dad was a milkman, and due to his normal early start he had gone to work. My mum decided that it would be a good time to leave Darren with his dad, while we searched the streets to find my dad and tell him what had happened. It took us a while, but eventually we found him. Following that, Mum took me back to my in-laws, not only to check on George, but also to shower before going back to the hospital. Darren was to be kept in for observations, due to his dilated pupil, as they were concerned that there was bleeding behind the eye.

On our return, Darren had been moved to a ward. I sat beside him, but the shock had hit me by this point. Both my mum and the ward nurse were concerned, so much so that the nurse called my doctor and made me an appointment. So, I left Darren again. I was rushed through, but Mum had to do all the talking, as I couldn't manage to string a sentence together. I just kept crying and asking why this had happened.

Dr Richards was comforting and prescribed me some antidepressant tablets, before advising my mum to take me home. I was assured that Darren would be home soon and I needed to rest. Unfortunately, rest was not happening. Every time I closed my eyes I would re-live the night.

After such a horrific night, I could never have imagined what lay ahead. I thought that I had already been through enough emotionally, yet more was to come.

We didn't return back to the house for many months, due to concerns over whether the attackers would return to finish the job. We tried different routes so that we could move, but the mortgage company would not help. Due to me being a housewife, we had no extra funds, so we eventually returned to our home.

The move back home was really difficult. Not only was I dealing with being a mum, but I also had to manage the traumatic impact that this attack had had on Darren. I had to be strong. Stupid little things would trigger something off in Darren, it was like someone had flicked a switch. His eyes would glaze over, and he would become someone else entirely. He wasn't the happy-go-lucky Darren I married. Instead, and this is the only way I could describe it, he became possessed. I didn't know what he would do. While on holiday I saw this look a couple of times, and I knew the best thing was to talk to him gently, explaining that all would be good, or to leave him on his own to deal with it. As much as it could scare me, I knew it wasn't his doing. I also knew it would only last a little while, and once he was 'back in the room' it was as though it never happened.

Although we would never discuss these incidents or dwell on them, thinking back I definitely should have spoken about it and demanded that Darren get better professional help. We were to come across several professionals during our journey, but one in particular comes to mind – as his failure to acknowledge Darren's state of mind, in my opinion, was criminal. His name was Dr. Pinto, and he was the psychiatrist on Darren's criminal compensation appeal board. Dr. Pinto determined that Darren's mental state was only "temporary" and he would be making a full recovery after 28 weeks. Well, 28 weeks came and went, and yes Darren was nowhere near to making a full recovery. I still find it difficult to get my head around these statements. I'd like to know who he studied to get that result.

Upon our return to the house, little things began to happen that would make me uneasy. For example, I once returned home from shopping with George. Before I could get to our front door, I was approached by a smartly dressed man, who had been sat outside the house in a car waiting for us. He did not introduce himself to me or let me know who he was, he just asked if I was Michelle. I began to panic. I was fumbling with my keys, trying to get in the house and get away from him. After getting the policeman in charge of our case involved in this, it turned out to be an innocent encounter by another officer, looking into something completely unrelated, but at the time it totally freaked me out.

It took a while, but eventually I started to feel that we could get back on with our lives, and I was determined to continue with this, especially for George's sake.

Darren's state of mind seemed to improve, especially once he returned to work, so we began to look towards adding to the family. In March 1998, our daughter Shannon was born. As much as I felt like Darren was ready for our family to increase, I have to be honest that I made the decision on my own. I felt Darren may have said no, due to a lack of confidence in himself. Before the attack, we had made plans to have more children, and there was no way I was going to allow those people to take our plans away from us.

The gremlin in Darren's head would pop out less and less as the years went on. Unbeknownst to me, this was because Darren was suppressing it subconsciously. This meant that it was never fully gone, and there were still some really dark days, with some that stuck out more than others. I know Darren has spoken of the day he left a rose on my car. This may sound like a very small thing to be talking about, but it truly was one of the lowest points of his eventual breakdown.

There were times when I wanted to escape this, but how could I leave him on his own? How could he be trusted with himself? Possibly the moment when I came closest to reaching my breaking point, was when we were out with my work colleagues for a birthday drink. Some random guy had bashed into the back of me, knocking me into a table. Now, although I do not drink any form of alcohol, I am more than aware of people who may have overdone it on the booze. However, I was not expecting Darren's reaction. He went berserk! I actually thought he was going to kill this guy that had bumped into me. I was absolutely furious with Darren, but I suppose this day was always going to happen. In the back of my mind, I had just been hoping that it wouldn't occur in public, and especially not in front of my friends.

If I am being completely honest, this was the time I hated what Darren had become. This was certainly not the man I married, and he was most certainly not the person he wanted to be. He was no longer the funny guy in the room, the guy that everyone wanted to be around. Instead, he was the guy we all wanted to avoid.

I spent that weekend mostly in tears, mostly wanting to punish Darren for ending a perfectly good evening with behaviour that belonged in the dark ages. I know now what had actually happened, as one of my workmates had witnessed the same as Darren, but only spoke to me about this when we returned to work on the Monday. However, I think that even after knowing the truth about that night I was still angry with Darren, and this was going to take some time to get over.

Watching Darren write this book has given me the greatest reward I could have wished for. I have seen him crying again, but this time it was for a positive reason. Darren now has it in him to be happy and enjoy every day, and for me that is so good to be around. I know that Darren has thanked many people for the role they have played in his life, and I would like to echo those sentiments, as they have also contributed to my life as well.

I know how tough this is going to be for my mum and dad to read, as we pretty much kept them away from all of this. Only now are they discovering what really happened. I needed them to be unaware of this, so that when we were together I could have my escape. So, thank you Mum and Dad. You are amazing.

I would also like to acknowledge my work colleagues, who supported me during my moments in need. On top of this, I would like to thank Jan, Tunai and Janet, all of whom really supported me once I finally broke down and confessed about my situation. I am not sure how things would have turned out without your love and guidance.

If I could pass one thing on to everyone who reads this book, it would be this: If you know someone who is suffering from a mental illness, please try hard not to lose faith in them. There really can be a light at the end of the tunnel, but they'll need your help to get there.

THAT NIGHT, MUM'S STORY

I heard the phone ring, and I remember looking at the clock. It was just after midnight. Pete answered the phone, but I could not hear who he was speaking to. However, the conversation didn't last for very long. Eventually he came back into the room. He had a strange look on his face, one that I had never seen before.

"Who was on the phone, Pete?" I asked

"It was Darren…we need to get over there, he's been hurt.'

At this point I couldn't possibly imagine the scale of what had happened, I just assumed Darren had slipped and hurt himself, or something along those lines. We both just tuned into autopilot, got ourselves dressed and made our way out to the car. I don't remember how long this all took, whether we rushed ourselves or just did things at the normal pace. All I remember is pulling up to the house, which was surrounded by police vehicles. There was tape cordoning off the entrance, and an officer standing by the drive.

Naturally, the first we did was to ask the officer if we could see Darren. His response was, "We have done all we can for him." Those words are the most haunting thing I have ever heard. They will stay with me forever. Now I was even more determined to get in, and the officer eventually let us through, but only to the doorway. There we were met by another officer, who led us upstairs.

I can remember, at the bottom of the stairs, seeing this machette type knife laying on the floor. It was huge. As we looked through into the living room, Darren was just sitting there huddled in a duvet on the floor. I do not know what was going through my mind at this stage, it was all too much to take in. We made our way upstairs as instructed, with the words of the policeman ringing in our ears. We sat with Wendy and George for what seemed like ages, but then we heard the ambulance arrive and the paramedics come in. The four of us just sat there, not saying much if anything at all. I could hear all the fuss going on downstairs, but could not really make out exactly what was happening.

Eventually they took Darren to the hospital, and Wendy went with him. Pete and I took George back home with us. The hours flew past, and I do not remember sleeping, but then it was just suddenly daylight and the morning had arrived. The day after the attack was my own dad's birthday, so I decided to give him a call and break the news to him. As I tried to tell him what had happened, my voice started to go all croaky. All he said was, "You have the same problem as me in the mornings, with my voice." Little did he know what devastating news I was about to tell him.

Once Darren was released from hospital, him, Wendy and George came to stay with us, so I decided to cook mince and potatoes. As I was peeling the onions it gave me a good excuse to have a good old cry. Teresa came to me and said, "It's hard being brave, Mum" which started me off crying again.

I can remember a constant flow of people coming to my house, all wanting to see Darren, and I can remember thinking please just leave us alone, but I could never had said anything. Every time I looked at Darren, I would ask myself, "Why you? You don't deserve this."

Our family friend Harvey arrived with his mate Dan, to see if Darren was ok, and within a few days Harvey's dad Frankie turned up too. Frankie brought some money with him, to help Darren get back on his feet. I always thought that this was a bit strange, but it was not my place to ask.

I do not know exactly how long Darren, Wendy and George were with us, but I think it was about 9 months. I just remember they stayed until they were ready to go home. I know it was such a difficult time, so Pete and I decided to send them away for a little holiday, with Teresa, Pete and Sam tagging along too.

When I reflect on the years that have passed, I can recollect how in the early days Darren was fearful of going out, as well as being in the house alone. I always felt that he was chasing something, whether it was a new job or a new business. He was always quite positive, and seemed to get on with his life, but he must have been carrying this around with him every day.

As a parent, you are always protective of your children, so the early days after the attack were tough for me and Pete. We felt utterly helpless. All we wanted to do was turn back the clock. Even now there are times when Pete and I sit and cry about "that night".

It was harder for Pete, I think. Being a man, he wanted revenge. I did too, to a degree, but my revenge would be aimed at the person that actually did it. I feel that the whole event has made me more aware of my surroundings, at all times. If someone can enter your home and do what they have done to Darren, it could happen to any of us anywhere.

I still have great trouble in going over any aspect of this, even after 20 odd years. It still upsets me just talking about it to anyone. I am not sure that I agree with Darren about the closure, now that I've got it all done, but hopefully it has helped Darren out.

At the end of the day, all parents want the best for their children. I can't turn back the clock, but I would do anything in my power to make things better for my son. I love you, Darren.

Mid and North East Essex Mind – Steph Shilton

Firstly, I would like to say how grateful I am that Darren has given me the opportunity to help raise awareness, not only about the work that Mind carries out but also general awareness about mental health.

Since 1985, Colchester Mind have been providing a range of mental health services driven by the needs of the local community. They are an independent charity, affiliated with the national charity Mind, with their own board of trustees and their own services.

In 2016, they merged with Mid-Essex Mind to form Mid and North East Essex Mind. Today they provide support for children from the age of 5 and adults of all ages. They have bases in Colchester, Clacton and Maldon, providing counselling, practical support, peer support and a dedicated Children and Young People's service. For more information about the services they provide please visit www.mnessexmind.org or call 01206 764600.

Having worked in the public health sector for 21 years in primary and secondary care, as a manager, I was fully aware of the need for far more mental health support.

When starting my long career, mental health patients did not seem to be offered priority care and community care was hardly in service. Over the past 10 years I have seen such a rapid increase in patients suffering with mental health issues, it has been quite heartbreaking.

I think the problem growth hit an all-time high around 2015. Since then the government have supported the NHS with much needed additional funding. However, we must never be complacent in the need for ongoing funding. We must ensure their goodwill continues.

I truly believe that the rise of social media has had a negative impact on the mental health of young people today. Self-harming, weight illnesses and young suicides may have been influenced by today's social media coverage. Until the government enforce tighter protocols, I suspect the dark side of the web will continue to tap into the vulnerable, which includes those prone to mental health illnesses. For me, that is very sad.

I am now a trustee for the Mid and North East Essex Mind. I thoroughly enjoy my role and will remain patient centered throughout. Mind offer amazing support to people suffering, right through to family members of all ages. Sometimes all you need to give someone is a lending ear and understanding, which is where we could all play a part in supporting a person who is struggling.

I never take for granted my position in life, and what I need to ensure I give back in my lifetime to others, I guess that comes from my semi-professional singing days. When I used to sing it could take you back to a place full of wonderful memories. I now only sing for charities, in the hope that my songs will help someone reach out for that happiness.

Mental illness can be a dreadful, lonely experience for sufferers, so please let's all reach out to those affected. Together, we can make the world a better place.

Steph Shilton
Peter&Steffi Shilton Consultancy Ltd
Tel: 07719 108 171
Email: steffi.shilto@yahoo.com

Useful Links and Organisations

MIND.

What we do Nationally: We provide advice and support to empower anyone experiencing a mental health problem. We campaign to improve services, raise awareness and promote understanding. **We won't give up** until everyone experiencing a mental health problem gets **support and respect**.

Every year, one in four of us will experience a mental health problem. But hundreds of thousands of people are still struggling.

We believe no-one should have to face a mental health problem alone. We'll listen, give you support and advice, and fight your corner.

© Mind. This information is published in full at mind.org.uk

You can contact Mind by using the following:

(www.mind.org.uk)

Mind infoline – Call 0300 123 3393 or text 86463

Email – info@mind.org.uk

Victim Support

About us

Victim Support (VS) is the independent charity for people affected by crime and traumatic events in England and Wales. Our specialist teams provide individual, independent, emotional and practical help to enable people to cope and recover from the effects of crime.

We're not part of the police, the courts or any other criminal justice agency. Our services are free and available to everyone, whether or not the crime has been reported and regardless of when it happened.

Last year we offered support to 814,000 people. With over 40 years' experience as the leading independent victims' charity, we know the impact that crime has on people's lives and what it takes to help them get their lives back on track.

We work locally to support people affected by crime, and campaign nationally to put their needs first, ensuring that they get the support they need and the respect they deserve. Together, we help people feel safer and find the strength to move forward after crime.

We need the generous support of members of the public to help even more people affected by crime and traumatic events. Your support will help us answer more calls, and give even more people the specialist support that they need to recover after crime.

Below is some useful information on what constitutes a crime, and how to deal with it.

What is a crime?

A crime is a deliberate act that causes physical or psychological harm, damage to or loss of property, and is against the law.

There are lots of different types of crime and nearly everyone will experience a crime at some point in their lives. One in five people were affected by crime last year; the equivalent of ten million people. It affects people from all backgrounds, locations and ages; more than one in ten children have been a victim of crime in the past year.

If you feel that you've been affected by crime in any way please contact us, even if you're not sure that the incident or event was a crime. You're not alone, and you can talk to us in confidence, regardless of when the crime took place or whether or not the police are involved.

Types of crime

There are lots of different types of crime, and people will react to crime differently. If you've been affected by crime and need support or information, please contact us.

Find out more about some of the specific types of crime below.

- Antisocial behaviour

  Antisocial behaviour is when you feel intimidated or distressed by a person's behaviour towards you.

- Arson

  Arson is when someone deliberately sets fire to someone else's property to damage it or to injure people.

- Burglary

  A burglary is when someone breaks into a building with the intention of stealing, hurting someone or committing unlawful damage.

- **Childhood abuse**

  Child abuse can happen in different ways, and can include neglect as well as physical, emotional and sexual abuse.

- **Crime abroad**

  Crime abroad covers any criminal offence that happens to you while outside England and Wales. This page also includes information about crime on cruise ships.

- **Cyber crime**

  The term cyber crime refers to a variety of crimes carried out online.

- **Domestic abuse**

  Domestic abuse describes negative behaviours that one person exhibits over another within families or relationships.

- **Fraud**

  Fraud is when someone tricks or deceives you to gain a dishonest advantage.

- **Hate crime**

  Hate crime is the term used to describe an incident or crime against someone based on a part of their identity.

- **Murder or manslaughter**

  Bereavement is a painful experience for anyone, but when you lose someone because of the violent actions of another person – through murder or manslaughter – it can be particularly devastating.

- <u>Rape and sexual assault</u>

  Find out more about rape and sexual assault and how you can get help.

- <u>Revenge porn</u>

  Revenge porn is when someone shares sexually explicit images or videos of another person without their consent.

- <u>Robbery</u>

  A robbery is when someone takes something from you with violence or threats – usually (but not always) in the street or another public place.

- <u>Sexual harassment</u>

  What is sexual harassment?

  Sexual harassment is any kind of unwanted behaviour of a sexual nature that makes you feel humiliated or intimidated, or that creates a hostile environment.

- <u>Stalking and harassment</u>

  Stalking is persistent and unwanted attention that makes you feel pestered and harassed.

- <u>Terrorism</u>

  Terrorist attacks are sudden and unpredictable and generally calculated to create a climate of fear or terror among the public.

  A terror attack can lead to an ongoing feeling of insecurity.

- <u>Violent crime</u>

  A violent crime is when someone physically hurts or threatens to hurt someone, and also includes crimes where a weapon is used.

Reporting a crime

If you've been a victim of crime, you'll need to decide whether or not to tell the police.

It's okay to feel unsure about this or worry about what will happen if you do. You might think that the police won't care. Maybe you've had a bad experience with the police in the past. Or perhaps you're worried that if you talk to the police, it will only make things worse.

If you decide to report to the police

There are positive reasons for reporting a crime. Remember that the police deal with all sorts of crime every day; they should treat everybody fairly and equally, and put your safety first.

If you report the crime, there's more chance that the offender will be caught or brought to justice for what they've done. The police also keep records of all reported crime and this information goes into government statistics and reports. These can change the way crime is dealt with by the police and other parts of the criminal justice system.

If you do decide to report a crime to the police then you'll automatically be put in touch with Victim Support. Remember that we'll give you help and support whether you decide to involve the police or not. Find out how to contact us.

How to report a crime

You can report a crime in several ways:

- If it's an emergency and the crime is still taking place, call <u>999</u> and ask for the police.

- **If it's not an emergency, do not call 999**. This doesn't mean the crime is not important – it just helps the police to make the best use of their resources. Many police forces use the 101 non-emergency number, so you can ring that number instead.

- You can go to your local police station and report the crime there. You can find the address and telephone number in the local telephone directory or online. Check what time your local police station is open, as not all stations are open all the time.

- You can contact Crimestoppers on 0800 555 111 if you want to remain anonymous.

- If you've experienced hate crime, you can also report the incident online through True Vision, or Victim Support's online portal if you live in Wales.

Here to help, whether or not you report the crime

Victim Support will help you whether you report the crime or not. Our service is confidential, and we won't pass on information to the police without your consent unless we think someone is at serious risk of harm and needs urgent help. Read more about our confidentiality policy.

Compensation for victims of violence crime

If you've been a victim of violent crime, you could be entitled to compensation under the government's criminal injuries compensation scheme. But to make a claim you must have reported the crime to the police as soon as possible after the event. If you don't report a violent crime, you may not be able to get compensation.

Time to Change

Time to Change is a growing movement of people changing how we all think and act about mental health.

Our aims are to:

- Improve public attitudes and behaviour towards people with mental health problems.

- Reduce the amount of discrimination that people with mental health problems report in their personal relationships, their social lives and at work.

- Make sure even more people with mental health problems can take action to challenge stigma and discrimination in their communities, in workplaces, in schools and online.

- Create a sustainable campaign that will continue long into the future.

Our voice is stronger and louder thanks to funding by the Department of Health, Comic Relief and the Big Lottery Fund, using National Lottery funding. Our campaign is run by charities **Mind** and **Rethink Mental Illness**, and thousands more organisations have joined us to make change happen.

Since Time to Change began in 2007, around 4.1 million adults in England have improved attitudes towards mental health problems – that's an improvement of 9.6% between 2008 and 2016. And more people than ever are able to be open about their mental health problems.

But we've still got a long way to go – too many people with mental health problems are still made to feel isolated, ashamed and worthless.

With the right support from those around them, people can recover and have equal opportunities in all areas of life.

Find out more by visiting (www.time-to-change.org.uk)

Booking Darren Barden for your event:

Visit: www.darrenbarden.com

Darren Barden is available for public speaking events.

To book Darren for your event, please go to:

www.DarrenBarden.com

In loving memory of my Grandad and my inspirational Auntie Jan who both are not here with me to share the good bits.

George (Grandad/Gramps) Billings – 8/10/1922 – 25/4/2000

Janet Pope – 16/11/1947 – 23/3/2018

"No longer dodging the undertaker Jan"

26538711R00085

Printed in Poland
by Amazon Fulfillment
Poland Sp. z o.o., Wrocław